Library of
Davidson College

FOREIGN BANKING AND INVESTMENT
IN THE UNITED STATES

By the same author

INTERNATIONAL BANKING AND FINANCE
INTERNATIONAL FINANCIAL MARKETS

Foreign Banking and Investment in the United States
Issues and Alternatives

FRANCIS A. LEES

A HALSTED PRESS BOOK

JOHN WILEY & SONS
New York

© Francis A. Lees 1976

All rights reserved. No part of this publication may be reproduced or transmitted, in any form or by any means, without permission

First published in the United Kingdom 1976 by
THE MACMILLAN PRESS LTD
London and Basingstoke

Published in the U.S.A.
by Halsted Press, a Division
of John Wiley & Sons, Inc.
New York.

Printed in Great Britain

Library of Congress Cataloging in Publication Data

Lees, Francis A
  Foreign banking and investment in the United States.

  "A Halsted Press book."
  Includes bibliographical references and index.
  1. Banks and banking, Foreign—United States.
2. Investments, Foreign—United States. I. Title.
HG2481.L44 1976   332.1′0973   76–4782
ISBN 0–470–15212–5

Contents

List of Tables vi
List of Abbreviations viii
Preface ix

I Extent of Foreign Bank Representation in U.S.
   1 The World of International Banking 3
   2 Extent of Foreign Bank Representation 9
   3 Factors Accounting for Expanded U.S. Presence 17
   4 National Representation Strategies 33

II Impact of Foreign Banking and Investment on U.S.
   5 Impact on U.S. Banking and Finance 45
   6 Multinational Portfolio Management 72

III Policy Issues
   7 Regulatory Issues and Alternatives 95
   8 Lessons from the U.K. Experience 126
   9 Problems and Issues 138

Appendix A. Statement of Condition of Foreign Bank Branches, Agencies, Investment Companies and Subsidiary Banks in the U.S., 31 December 1974   145
Appendix B. Summary of New York Superintendent's Denial of Barclays Acquisition of Long Island Trust Company   147
Notes 151
Selected References 155
Index 159

List of Tables

1-1 Principal Factors Relating to International Banking Role of Ten Major Countries — 6
1-2 Global Network of Overseas Branches and Agencies, 1973 — 7
2-1 States which Authorise Operation of Foreign Bank Activities in their Jurisdiction — 13
2-2 Foreign Banking Representation in the United States by Type of Office and by State, 1975 — 15
3-1 Assets and Liabilities of Foreign-Owned U.S. Banking Institutions as of 31 October 1973 — 23
3-2 Growth of Assets held by Foreign Banks in New York, 1950–73 — 25
3-3 State Chartered Subsidiaries of Foreign Banks as Percentage of Industry in California — 30
3-4 State Chartered Subsidiaries of Foreign Banks, Domestic Deposits, Rank, and Percentage of State Deposits — 31
5-1 Deposits in Commercial Banks Facing Potential Competition from Foreign Banks, by State, 31 December 1973 — 52
5-2 Analysis of Exposure to Potential International Competition, by State, 31 December 1973 — 55
5-3 Foreign Ownership of Money Market Assets in New York, 1973–74 — 59
5-4 Size Comparison of New York Money Market and International Asset Categories, 1973–74 — 60
5-5 Reserve Requirements against Deposit Liabilities in Selected States — 67
6-1 Calculation of Expected Return and Dispersion of Return from an Investment in U.S. by a Foreign Bank — 73

LIST OF TABLES

6-2	Risk–Return Relationships on Domestic, Foreign, and Global Investment Portfolio	75
6-3	Foreign Direct Investments in the United States	78
6-4	Estimated Deployment of Oil Producer Funds, 1974	89
8-1	Deposit Structure in U.K. Banks, 1974	127
8-2	Comparison of International Banking Role of United Kingdom and United States, 1973	133

List of Abbreviations

BBIL	Barclays Bank International Limited
BBL	Barclays Bank Limited
BHC	bank holding company
CD	certificate of deposit
FDIC	Federal Deposit Insurance Corp.
IET	Interest Equalization Tax
IMF	International Monetary Fund
JFK	John F. Kennedy
LIT	Long Island Trust Co., New York
NYSE	New York Stock Exchange
OFDI	Office of Foreign Direct Investments
OPEC	Organization of Petroleum Exporting Countries

Preface

Banking has become one of the most interesting sectors in the American business system. Several factors explain the recently acquired dynamics of the banking field including the presence of a new breed of competitive leaders, the perception of opportunities in semi-isolated regional markets, government regulation and controls that strait-jacket free competition, and a minor assault from abroad on what previously have been well-entrenched positions. In addition to providing incentives for reconsidering the role of existing regulatory agencies, the new dynamics contain possibilities of new entrants into the game of regulation. For example, the Securities and Exchange Commission is watching the securities activities of American commercial banks with great attention.

My own interest in the subject of foreign banking in the U.S. extends back into a prior study concerning the role of the United States in international banking. In that study major attention was given to the activities and organisational strategies of American banks overseas. However, it was also necessary to include a detailed description and analysis of the role and status of foreign banks in the United States.

Events during the past two years have heightened interest in the expansion of foreign banking in the United States. Attitudes in the U.S. appear to have changed somewhat given the realisation by informed Americans that many foreign banks rank closely with domestic institutions in size and competitiveness. Policy changes may be around the corner, which adds to the practical interest of this study. The recently enacted Foreign Investment Study Act of 1974 attests to the keen interest of Congress in such matters. From a practical standpoint the question of the future role of the United States as an international financial center, the financial intermediation of internationally lendable funds, and the viability of the new and evolving international monetary system all focus importantly on the activities of foreign banks in the United States. Moreover, analysis of the role of foreign banks in the U.S. financial markets sheds further light on the nature of deficiencies in domestic financial market structure and operation.

A study such as the following requires considerable information and expert opinion that is not published or readily available. Therefore, I wish to express my grateful appreciation to the persons who generously supplied me with information, or shared with me their own insights into trends and relationships in the field of foreign banking. These include the following: Fred B. Ruckdeschel, Secretary, Federal Reserve System Steering Committee on International Banking Regulation; Donald E. Pearson, Superintendent of Banks, California; Harry W. Albright, Superintendent of Banks, New York; Joseph Sharkey, Assistant Deputy Superintendent of Banks, New York; Bertwing C. Mah, Director of Research, California State Banking Department; Paul H. Starkey, Assistant Commissioner of Banks and Trust Companies, State of Illinois; Dr George W. Coleman, Member Legislative Task Force, American Bankers Association; Paul Horvitz, Director of Research, Federal Deposit Insurance Corporation; Dr Nicholas Bruck, Economist, Inter-American Development Bank; Dr Maximo Eng, Department of Economics and Finance, St Johns University; and Dr William Ford, Director of Economic Research, American Bankers Association.

All residual errors accrue to the author.

August 1975   FRANCIS A. LEES

I
EXTENT OF FOREIGN BANK REPRESENTATION IN U.S.

1 The World of International Banking

> I am not an Athenian or a Greek,
> but a citizen of the world.
>
> Socrates

During the decade of the 1960s banks in the United States assumed a prominent role in international finance, based on the development of overseas branch offices and acquisitions of ownership in foreign subsidiaries. In the 1970s the U.S. prominence in international banking continues, but in somewhat different format. The United States has become a magnet, attracting foreign banking institutions and foreign investors. This volume focuses on the second aspect of the international banking role of the U.S., namely the growth of foreign bank representation and operations in America.

A. LEADERSHIP IN INTERNATIONAL BANKING

What makes a country prominent in international banking? What conditions are necessary for domestic financial institutions to become interested in overseas representation? At what stage of development is a national economy likely to offer advantages for direct foreign bank representation in its money and credit markets? Why are some countries more attractive exporters of foreign banking representation, while other countries tend to attract foreign banking representation?

Why has the 'friendly invasion' of foreign banks into the U.S. followed closely on the heels of growing involvement by American banks in international banking? Are these two developments largely independent, or are they connected?

A number of factors enter into determining how important any single country will be in international banking. These include the extent of that country's participation in world export-import trade, the importance of that country as a source of lendable funds, the strength of the country's currency, and the size and managerial efficiency of its banking institutions.

Numerous intangibles enter into the picture insofar as leadership in international banking is concerned. How cooperative are government agencies in providing an open, liberal, and efficient regulatory environment? Are banking institutions regulated to an excessive extent? Is the national attitude toward banking liberal, or is it only tolerant, or even dominated by an unfriendly populist sentiment? To what extent is government support of banking institutions sufficient to give domestic banks a competitive edge over foreign banks?

B. MAJOR COUNTRIES

In the following table are some comparative statistics of ten countries that are leaders in international banking. At the top of the table are listed the United Kingdom and United States, who play a leading role due to their long-standing importance in foreign trade, their broad and efficient money markets, the sophistication of banking and other financial institutions, and their leadership in foreign business investment. These two countries stand apart in terms of the range of financial services they uniquely provide for the rest of the world.

Table 1-1 also includes four leading countries, Germany, Japan, Switzerland and Canada. Together with the U.S. and U.K. these four countries provide a major part of the international banking framework in the world today, including a large network of foreign branches and agencies (Column 7 in Table 1-1). Interestingly, these countries have developed their international banking facilities along somewhat different lines, and as a result of differing specialisations. Germany has developed into a leading international banking country through rapid growth in foreign trade, a strong domestic currency, an ability to generate balance of payments surpluses which finance foreign lending and bond issue activity, and a sizeable inflow of foreign business investment which has provided large German banks with important business contacts around the globe. Japan's leadership in international banking stems equally from rapid growth in foreign trade. However, in many other areas Japan's leadership in global banking differs from

Germany's. Japan has borrowed heavily from overseas areas (especially the U.S.) and its capital market has only recently been opened to foreign borrowers. Japan's leadership has resulted in part from close coordination between banks and the non-banking business sector, both at home and overseas. Moreover, government authorities have supported the overseas expansion of Japanese banking.

Switzerland's prominence in global banking reflects the well-developed and efficiently managed Swiss capital market, the conservative management of the Swiss monetary system, and the stable value of the Swiss franc in the world currency markets. The Swiss have been adroit and successful money and investment portfolio managers, and this has attracted non-resident funds into Swiss banks. Overseas representation of Swiss banks is moderate, but focused carefully along the lines of greatest efficiency. Hence the Swiss banks have become important factors in underwriting and securities activities in New York and in other financial centres. The Canadian banks have built a substantial foreign exchange and international banking business based in part on their open economy (a high proportion of foreign trade to national income). In addition, Canada has received substantial long-term capital inflows from U.S. business investment and sale of bond issues in New York. The Canadian banks customarily hold a large amount of foreign currency as a reserve against foreign currency deposits. These funds in turn are invested in the New York money market, the Eurocurrency market, or swapped into Canadian dollars for domestic lending. The Canadian banks have built up a sizeable number of foreign branches and agencies, as well as established numerous subsidiary banking institutions in foreign countries.

The data in Table 1-1 also refers to four countries that play an important role in international banking. These include France, Italy, the Netherlands, and Belgium. All four of these countries enjoy a substantial base of foreign trade, hold considerable foreign exchange and gold reserves, and participate actively in the Eurocurrency markets.

A more comprehensive picture of the international banking linkages between countries and regions of the world is provided in Table 1-2. Here we can observe the closeness of linkage as

Table 1-1

Principal Factors Relating to International Banking Role of Ten Major Countries

Country	Mdse. Exports	Foreign Bond Issues	Official Reserves	Foreign Exchange Held by Banks	Eurocurrency Deposits in Banks	Domestic Banks Number of Banks	Number of Branch-Agencies
	1	2	3	4	5	6	7
Major Centres							
U.S.	71.3	1,334.8	14.6	0.9	—	101	691
U.K.	30.5	141.9	6.9	—	59.8	21	2,242
Leading Countries							
Germany	67.5	422.0	33.8	9.7	3.9	5	14
Japan	36.9	635.8	12.7	11.0	7.5	13	94
Switzerland	9.5	984.1	7.4	—	8.5	10	29
Canada	26.2	20.4	6.2	13.1	8.1	5	237
Important Countries							
France	36.6	19.5	8.1	—	19.1	22	230
Italy	22.2	197.8	6.2	25.3	18.8	5	21
Netherlands	24.0	15.4	5.7	9.3	6.4	4	64
Belgium	22.4	110.7	4.7	12.1	14.8	5	24

Notes: Columns 1, 3, 4, 5 expressed in billions of U.S. dollars. Column 2 is expressed in million of U.S. dollars.
1. Year 1973. 2. Year 1972, except for U.K. where figure reflects 1971 bond issues.
3. As of April 1974. 4. Yearend 1973 (except for U.S. where data are for first quarter 1970).
5. Yearend 1972. 6. Data refer to number of banks and foreign offices in 1973.

Sources: IMF, *International Financial Statistics*; OECD, *Financial Statistics*; Bank for International Settlements, *Annual Reports*; Bank of England, *Quarterly Bulletin*; and *Bankers Almanac & Yearbook, 1972–73*.

Table 1-2

Global Network of Overseas Branches and Agencies 1973

Country of Origin	U.S.	U.K.	France	Germany	Switz.	Neth.	Other Europ	Carib.	Panama	Other Latin Amer.	Japan	Hong Kong	Singapore Malaya	Other Far East	Mid-East	Africa	Total
U.S. (101)	—	58	20	27	15	9	48	158	32	161	22	23	15	64	21	18	691
U.K. (21)	15	—	6	8	7	2	62	73	—	94	6	37	78	1469	80	305	2242
France (22)	3	9	—	9	8	2	24	2	2	49	2	3	3	34	6	74	230
Germany (5)	2	—	—	—	—	—	2	—	1	3	1	1	1	3	1	—	14
Switz. (10)	5	9	2	1	—	2	3	4	—	1	2	—	—	—	6	2	29
Netherl. (4)	2	2	—	—	1	—	—	5	1	29	3	4	3	5	11	—	64
Italy (5)	4	2	—	—	—	1	1	—	—	1	1	—	1	—	—	18	21
Other Europe (15)	1	11	27	6	4	—	10	—	—	16	—	3	—	—	11	1	97
Canada (5)	13	17	1	1	—	—	4	164	—	35	—	—	—	—	—	—	237
Japan (13)	39	12	1	5	—	—	2	—	—	9	—	6	4	16	1	—	94
Australia (9)	—	19	1	—	—	—	—	—	—	—	—	—	2	41	—	12	63
Other Far East (32)	11	32	1	2	2	—	1	—	3	2	14	33	101	37	16	—	262
Latin America (4)	11	1	—	1	—	—	—	—	3	6	1	—	—	—	—	—	25
Caribbean (3)	7	1	4	—	—	—	—	—	—	48	—	—	—	—	—	—	59
Mid-East (10)	5	5	2	3	—	—	—	1	—	—	—	—	—	—	39	—	57
Africa (8)	—	6	—	—	—	—	—	—	—	—	—	—	—	—	1	6	15
Total (267)	118	184	65	63	37	16	157	407	42	454	52	110	208	1669	182	436	4200

Note: Figures in brackets refer to number of domestic banks with overseas branches and agencies.

Source: *Bankers Almanac & Yearbook, 1972–73.*

measured by number of internationally oriented banks of countries of origin that operate overseas branch and agency offices, as well as the number of such offices, and their location in host countries. In 1973 some 267 internationally oriented banks operated 4,200 overseas branches and agencies. These figures largely exclude the banking offices of overseas subsidiary banks.

2 Extent of Foreign Bank Representation

> And dar'st thou, then
> To beard the lion in his den,
> The Douglas in his hall?
>
> Sir Walter Scott

A. SCOPE OF FOREIGN BANK ACTIVITIES IN U.S.

The expansion of foreign bank operations in the United States has been impressive. Over 150 foreign banks now operate representative offices, agencies, branches and subsidiaries in the United States, representing all major European countries, Canada, Japan and a growing number of less developed countries. At yearend 1974 foreign banks held U.S. assets in excess of $56 billion. The range of operations of foreign banks has broadened in recent years, and now includes lending in the domestic credit markets, retail banking, money market activities, stock market transactions, and securities underwriting.

A basic theme underlying this volume is that the recent growth of foreign bank activities in the United States is only part of a broad pattern and trend which embraces the internationalisation of global business, specifically including the flow of foreign investment into the United States. In the period 1960–72 foreign investment in the United States expanded from $40.8 billion to $148.6 billion. Foreign investment entering the United States takes three principal forms; portfolio investment, direct investment, and short-term investment in liquid assets. All three are intimately related to the increasing role of foreign bank operations in the U.S.

Foreign banks employ several organisational forms in their operations in the U.S., including the representative office, agency, branch, and the corporate subsidiary. In theory the representative office does not perform banking functions, but may facilitate banking transactions through local correspondents. The primary functions of representative offices appear to be to provide information concerning the parent bank, to serve as liaison with respect to various activities of the parent bank, and to function as an intermediary in providing information to American companies interested in offshore financing.

The agency and branch forms are permitted in several states, given the approval of the State Superintendent of Banks and the Banking Board. Generally, a licensing requirement must be satisfied. While an agency may appear to resemble a branch, there are several significant differences. Agencies may not accept deposits, although they do maintain 'credit balances' which are claims of customers derived from financing foreign trade and other transactions. Branches are empowered to conduct a general banking business, including the right to accept deposits. In New York branches and agencies are licensed annually.

Foreign-owned bank subsidiaries and trust companies generally operate in a manner similar to that of domestic commercial banks. These subsidiaries may be eligible for Federal Reserve membership and must have deposit insurance coverage by the Federal Deposit Insurance Corporation. Several New York chartered trust companies confine their activities to corporate agency functions. The California chartered subsidiaries of foreign banks operate along general banking and retail lines.

New York Banking Law provides for the chartering of investment companies which engage in loan and investment activities. These companies generally emphasise financing high-risk trade or participate in venture capital schemes. The investment companies are not permitted to accept deposits but may maintain credit balances.

B. DEVELOPMENT AND GROWTH

The following discussion focuses on development and growth of foreign banks in New York. In subsequent sections we analyse more recent expansion of foreign banking across the United States.

The development of foreign banking in the United States can

be traced to the mid-nineteenth century, when the U.S. was emerging from pre-industrial status and receiving substantial foreign investments that balanced off a negative foreign trade position. In the early years foreign bank representation was confined to New York, the chief port of entry and the financial centre of the nation. The Bank of Montreal established an office in New York City in 1859, and in 1879 the Hongkong and Shanghai Banking Corporation became the first British bank to gain representation in New York. By the turn of the century several other foreign banks were established in New York (including Barclays Bank DCO), and several additional foreign institutions were preparing for entry.

By 1911 the growth of foreign banking in New York had developed to a point where the State Banking Department initiated a study of the role of foreign banks, which resulted in an amendment to the Banking Law. This amendment provided for the licensing of foreign bank agencies to engage in the business of making loans, buying or selling bills of exchange, issuing letters of credit, receiving money for transmission, or transmitting funds by draft or check. By 1913 there were twenty-one foreign banks operating agencies in New York. During the war years (1914–18) the number of agencies stabilised, but their volume of operations declined. World War I left an indelible mark on international finance and the incentives for foreign bank representation in the United States. The U.S. rose to a position of prominence in international finance, U.S. merchandise exports and loans became a key aspect of world business, and the dollar became a respected and sought-after international currency.

The decade of the 1920s witnessed a surge in the international creditor status of the U.S., as foreign dollar bonds were sold to American investors in larger amounts in each successive year. Foreign banks were attracted to New York to better service their customers. By the late 1920s foreign bond placements were declining in amount, and the worldwide depression of the 1930s was followed by a sharp drop in export-import trade. In the period 1929–32 U.S. merchandise trade declined to one-third of its 1929 peak. The sharp decline in foreign trade and international lending did not result in the wholesale closing of foreign banking offices in New York. By the end of the decade there were almost as many foreign bank agencies operating in

New York as in the late 1920s.

With the outbreak of World War II new problems emerged in the supervision of foreign bank agencies. In December 1941 the New York Superintendent of Banks took possession of the six Japanese agencies operating in New York, as well as the four Italian agencies. Prior to this a Presidential Executive Order had frozen all Italian funds in the United States. Under federal law the licenses of the Japanese and Italian agencies were replaced by supervision of the Alien Property Custodian, and payments were effected to recognised claimants.

The 1950s represented an expansion phase for foreign bank agencies in New York. In 1951 New York amended the Banking Law to specifically permit foreign bank agencies to maintain credit balances for the account of others. By yearend 1951 twenty foreign bank agencies, six foreign owned trust companies, and three investment companies were operating in New York. These foreign banking interests held combined assets of $1.3 billion. The decade of the 1950s was important in several respects. First, foreign bank agencies enjoyed an impressive growth in resources. Second, U.S. banks began to develop an awakening interest in overseas banking opportunities. Finally, American banks met increasing resistance in several countries that complained about the lack of reciprocity in the U.S. Banks in these countries (including Brazil, Uruguay, and the Philippines) had complained that the United States authorities, especially in New York State, did not provide reciprocal opportunities to establish branches.

As a result, internationally oriented banks in New York initiated discussion pointed at legislation that would permit foreign banks to establish branches in New York. A foreign branching bill was proposed in 1959 by the Chase Manhattan Bank and the First National City Bank of New York. Numerous groups favoured passage of a branching bill, which was expected to enhance the prestige of New York and to permit it to increase its role as an international financial centre. The bill was signed into law and became effective in 1961. Five foreign banks quickly converted their New York agencies to branch status. By yearend 1963 twenty-two foreign banks were operating New York agencies, and nineteen had obtained branch licenses.

Table 2-1

States which Authorise Operation of Foreign Bank Activities in their Jurisdiction

	Agency	Branch	Affiliate	Branch or Agency
New York	Yes[a]	Yes[a]	Yes	Yes
California	Yes	Yes[b]	Yes	
Illinois	—	Yes	Yes	
Massachusetts	Yes	Yes	Yes	
Pennsylvania	—	Yes[c]	Yes	
Washington	Yes[a]	Yes[a]	—	Yes
Oregon	Yes	Yes	—	
Florida	—	—	—[d]	
Hawaii	Yes	—	Yes	

[a] Branch or agency permitted, but not both.
[b] FDIC insurance is required on domestic deposits in branches of foreign banks (which is not available under federal law).
[c] The Pennsylvania provision for foreign bank branches is somewhat restrictive and a more liberal chartering provision was proposed early in 1974.
[d] Florida recently enacted legislation prohibiting acquisitions of Florida banks by foreign interests. However, immediately prior to this a Canadian banking institution had acquired the stock of a Florida based bank.

Sources: Correspondence of the author with State Banking Superintendents, and a clipping file maintained on state regulation of foreign banking.

C. STATES OF LOCATION

The preceding section focused on the development of foreign bank activities in New York. However, these institutions are represented in a number of other states. Nevertheless, New York offices account for over 80 per cent of foreign bank resources in the U.S. and the range of activities undertaken from New York offices is the widest in scope.

Eight states expressly provide for the licensing and operation of foreign owned banking offices in their respective jurisdictions. In so doing these states have treated representative offices, subsidiaries, agencies and branches of foreign banks as separate and distinct entities requiring different supervision. In most states (with the exception of California) foreign banks may establish a representative office without going through the formality of obtaining a license.

In general state chartered subsidiaries of foreign banks have been organised and supervised in a manner similar to that applying to domestic banks. Nonbank subsidiaries of foreign banks generally are treated according to the incorporation laws and business practice codes that apply. New York, California, and Massachusetts appear to be the most permissive, in that these states allow almost any kind of foreign bank operation including agency, branch or banking subsidiary. California law requires that branches of foreign banks provide FDIC insurance on domestic source deposits. Since this deposit insurance is not available by Federal statute, foreign branches cannot be established. However, agencies in California are authorised to accept deposits from foreign sources.

A few states prohibit foreign bank branches (Delaware, Texas, and Vermont), while others (Connecticut, Florida, Maryland, New Jersey and Ohio) will not admit foreign bank offices in any form. The remaining states, approximately three dozen, have enacted no statutory provisions which specifically refer to the establishment of foreign bank operations in their respective jurisdictions.

Despite the fact that foreign banks must contend with a heterogeneity of state regulations and laws, approximately 160 foreign banking institutions have established direct representation in the United States. Table 2-2 outlines the number of foreign banking units in the United States at midyear 1975, by state of location. At that time foreign banks were operating at least 142 representative offices, 73 agencies, 81 branches, and 36 banking subsidiaries. In addition, 49 nonbank subsidiaries of foreign banking institutions were operating in at least eleven states. While the importance of foreign banks in New York tends to overshadow their activities in other states, we should note that in recent years foreign banks have been expanding

Table 2-2

Foreign Banking Representation in the United States
by Type of Office and by State
1975

	Representative Offices	Agencies	Branches	Banking Subsidiary	Non-bank Subsidiary
California	14	37[a]	—[a]	15	8[b]
Colorado	—	—	—	—	1
District of Columbia	6	—	—	—	1[c]
Florida	2	—	—	1	—
Georgia	—	—	—	—	2[c]
Hawaii	—	1	—	1	1[c]
Illinois	14	—	15	3	4[c]
Maryland	—	—	—	—	1[c]
Massachusetts	—	—	1	—	2[c]
New York	97	35	52[e]	16	27[d]
Oregon	—	—	2	—	—
Pennsylvania	—	—	—	—	1[c]
Texas	8	—	—	—	—
Washington	1	—	4	—	—
Wisconsin	—	—	—	—	1[c]
U.S. Virgin Islands	—	—	7[f]	—	—
Totals	142	73	81	36	49

[a] Represents 37 agencies operated by 36 different foreign banks. California law does not permit branches of foreign banks to accept deposits from U.S. residents without FDIC insurance, which is not available to them. However, these banking offices are permitted to accept deposits from non-residents without deposit insurance. This places these banking offices in a dual (agency-branch) status.
[b] Principally California branches of New York based securities affiliates of foreign banks.
[c] Branch of New York based merchant bank or securities affiliate.
[d] Includes 21 securities affiliates and 6 specialty finance companies.
[e] This includes 52 branches of 31 foreign banks.
[f] This includes 7 branches of 3 foreign banks.

Source: New York State Superintendent of Banks; California Superintendent of Banks; and *American Banker*.

their activities in states such as California and Illinois, and that in future we might expect to see a wider geographic base of operations.

3 Factors Accounting for Expanded U.S. Presence

> 'A slow sort of country!' said the Queen.
> 'Now, here, you see, it takes all the running you can do, to keep in the same place. If you want to get somewhere else, you must run at least twice as fast as that!'
>
> *Alice in Wonderland*

In this chapter we review the advantages inherent in direct U.S. representation, and point to the factors responsible for the expansion of foreign banking operations in the United States. A concluding section of this chapter analyses the development of foreign banking on a quantitative basis, and traces the expansion of foreign banks in several of the states which have been important growth centres.

A. ADVANTAGES PECULIAR TO U.S. LOCATION

A century ago foreign banks were only beginning to establish representative offices and agency operations in New York. In the most recent decade foreign banks have rediscovered the U.S. as an attractive locus for doing business. Conditions have changed over the past century and the advantages inherent in establishing and developing U.S. banking offices today are quite different from what they were in the nineteenth century.

Numerous advantages currently accrue to foreign banking institutions with U.S. representation. These may be summarised as follows:

1. Economic advantages, including the substantial volume of foreign trade, and strength of the dollar as an

international currency.
2. Size of the U.S. banking and credit markets.
3. Splintered structure of U.S. banking (state cells, restrictions on branching, and dual federal-state chartering).
4. Competitive reaction of foreign banks to the aggressive global strategy of major U.S. banks.
5. Dynamics of the U.S. situation, including opportunities for bank holding company expansion, and extension of banks into near bank activities.

B. FACTORS RESPONSIBLE FOR EXPANSION OF FOREIGN BANKS

The discussion in this section focuses on the financial service areas that appear to offer favourable opportunities to foreign banks in the United States. We should note that in some cases these financial service areas have permitted rapid internal growth of existing branches, agencies and subsidiaries of foreign banking corporations. In other cases the opportunities seen by foreign banks in these financial service areas have induced them to establish operating offices *de novo*.

1. CORPORATE SERVICES

Foreign corporations have become an important part of the business fabric in the United States, and their own home country banks have been quick to perceive the advantages inherent in locating offices in the U.S. that can service these firms. An accelerating inflow of foreign business capital has resulted in the accumulation of nearly $20 billion (1974) of direct investment in the U.S. by non-resident companies. Seventy-three per cent of this direct investment is owned by European companies, including the major industrial giants in the United Kingdom, Germany, the Netherlands, and Switzerland. Canadian companies account for twenty-three per cent of direct investment in the U.S. Foreign banks cannot ignore the opportunities for business development, nor the competitive implications of not being ready to service their home country companies in the U.S. For purely competitive reasons major foreign banks, especially those in countries with substantial business investments in the United States, have been under pressure to follow their corporate customers.

The incentives for foreign banks to enter the U.S. has been further reinforced by the need to provide financial services for corporate customers unacquainted with doing business in the United States. A close relationship between the parent bank and parent company in the home country provides the basis for continued financial service relationships between the U.S. subsidiaries of both parties. The U.S. office of the foreign bank is familiar with local business practices, is in close contact with U.S. financial institutions, and can provide information on business conditions in the United States. The officers in charge of U.S. branches and agencies of foreign banks generally have a good understanding of the banking needs of the American subsidiary, and are familiar with the management methods and operations of the foreign parent and its overseas subsidiaries.

Foreign banks operating in the United States have not been able to depend on servicing American subsidiaries of their home country customers for all or nearly all of their business volume. The number of subsidiaries of foreign corporations is relatively limited, and their banking business has been vigorously competed for by domestic banks in the U.S. Consequently, foreign banks have attempted to develop bank service relationships with U.S. corporations.

U.S. corporations might be expected to place some business with the American branch or affiliate of a foreign bank whose head office services the overseas subsidiary of the U.S. company. This expectation has been realised, and corporate treasurers in the U.S. have placed deposits or funnelled loans through American banking offices of foreign banks. In some cases the placement of business with the U.S. office of the foreign bank is in anticipation of developing close account relationships and loan funds for overseas affiliates of American companies. For this reason a number of foreign banks have been able to develop a sizeable base of working capital lending with U.S. companies that have operations abroad.

Foreign banks have developed good working relationships with U.S. companies for a variety of reasons, including the ability to finance the export and import business of U.S. firms on favourable terms. Additional services provided by foreign banks to U.S. corporate clients include providing information on money and loan market conditions and foreign exchange market developments.

2. MONEY MARKET OPERATIONS

The New York offices of foreign banks have long been recognised as important participants in U.S. money market operations. The Canadian agencies in New York have been active in the market for call loans to securities dealers and brokers. Nearly all foreign banks have been active in the federal funds market, and after introduction of the negotiable certificate of deposit (CD) in 1961 subsidiaries and branches of foreign banks have obtained money market funds by sale of CDs to corporate treasurers.

In June 1975 the Sanwa Bank Ltd. of Osaka announced it would begin to offer large negotiable certificates of deposit through its Chicago branch. The Sanwa Bank officials indicated that this would broaden the base of U.S. funding operations and support an extension of its U.S. banking business.[1]

Operations in the New York money market tend to 'complete' the global capacity of foreign banking institutions to shift sources of funds and to maximise the return on their liquid portfolios. Through U.S. offices foreign banks can arbitrage money market funds between New York, London, the continental Eurocurrency centres, Canada, and more outlying money centres.

3. DOLLAR SOURCING

Over the past quarter century the dollar has been an attractive and sought after currency by international bankers, traders, and investors. Consequently, a major consideration in foreign bank decisions to establish U.S. banking offices has been the objective of developing a base from which to supply the dollar requirements of the parent bank. In addition, U.S. banking offices provide a ready depository and clearing centre for dollar operations of the parent institution. A foreign bank's office or affiliate in New York may be asked to extend overdrafts to other units of the parent bank within prescribed limits. If corresponding funds have not been received by cable or telex instructions from parent bank headquarters the New York office acquires a 'due from' balance against an overseas affiliate of the parent bank, or the parent bank's head office. The New York office may be instructed to provide credit facilities to affiliates or branches outside the U.S. that must refinance their own loans to customers with dollars. An important advantage of a dollar base is the ability to operate in the exchange market after the head office (in Europe or elsewhere) has closed for the day.

Immediate access to the New York financial markets permits the U.S. office or affiliate to invest net dollar balances acquired during the day for own account or for the account of head office. Such funds can be invested in any sector of the money market, or in government securities. Finally, a U.S. office can operate in either direction in the money market, i.e., it can serve as a ready source of liquidity when the parent bank is experiencing a credit squeeze or it can lay off excess funds in the money market.

4. RETAIL BANKING

While foreign banks operating in New York have confined their operations largely to wholesale banking, there are important exceptions. Several foreign banks in New York have had a strong appeal with ethnic groups. The branches of Puerto Rican banks and the subsidiaries of Israeli banks are important cases in point. These branches and subsidiaries offer a wide range of retail banking services including personal checking, savings accounts, and consumer loans.

In California foreign owned subsidiary banks are heavily retail oriented. California law permits unlimited branching, and several foreign bank affiliates have substantial branch networks and deposit totals approaching the one billion dollar mark.

5. SECURITIES MARKET LINKAGES

A major consideration for foreign banks developing their representation in the United States has been the desire to extend the geographic sphere of their underwriting and securities trading activities. In recent years over a dozen foreign banking institutions have established securities affiliates in the U.S. or acquired ownership in existing securities firms. In a number of cases foreign banks jointly own a New York based securities affiliate.

Several foreign banks that operate through securities affiliates in the U.S. also conduct commercial banking operations (through branch offices). This gives these foreign institutions an advantage over American banks, which are prohibited from simultaneously engaging in investment banking and commercial banking by the Glass-Steagall Act. We return to this question in Chapter 4 where we discuss organisational strategies of foreign banks in the U.S., and in Chapter 6 where we discuss the investment banking and portfolio management activities of foreign banks in further detail.

C. SOURCES AND USES OF FUNDS

At the international level banks generally find it difficult to establish stable sources of deposit funds. At home banks can rely on deposits provided by regular customers, and supplement this source with funds from the domestic money market. Another important source of funds is the international money market (Eurodollar deposits). However, this market is less stable, and offers lower profit margins when end uses of funds are considered.

Participants in the money markets, especially at the international level, are highly sophisticated, and this increases the problem bankers encounter in attempting to build dependable deposit sources of lendable funds. Foreign banks operating in the U.S. have encountered these problems, as have American banks that have established branches overseas. When operating outside their home country banks often rely on funds supplied from the head office of the parent institution. However, in recent years there have been increased pressures working against this solution in the form of limits imposed on capital inflows of this type, either for balance of payments reasons or due to the need to control domestic credit creation. Finally, banks in foreign countries attempt to supplement their lending resources by drawing on local money market funds, often in the form of borrowing in the interbank market (in the U.S., federal funds). Where other money market sectors are sufficiently developed foreign banks will endeavour to tap these sources as well.

Foreign banks operating in the United States tend to reflect these funding difficulties. In 1973 close to 40 per cent of the resources of foreign banks came from foreign sources (Table 3-1). These funds are derived primarily from the home offices

Table 3-1

Assets and Liabilities of Foreign-Owned U.S. Banking Institutions as of 31 October 1973

Billions of dollars

Assets		Liabilities	
Commercial and industrial credits	15.4	Deposits and other liabilities Nonbank	
Of which		From U.S.	5.5
To U.S.	11.8	From Foreign	3.6
To Foreign	3.6	Bank (non-affiliated)	
Money Market Assets		From U.S.	6.8
Interbank loans and securities		From Foreign Due to parent bank and	0.5
Loans to U.S. Banks[a]	4.4	other affiliated institu-	
Loans to Foreign Banks	1.1	tions	
U.S. Government agency securities	1.5	In U.S. Foreign	3.4 10.1
Due from parent bank and		Clearing balances	2.0
other affiliated institutions		Other liabilities	2.3
In U.S.	2.9	Capital and reserves	0.9
Foreign	4.2		
Clearing balances	3.0		
Other assets	2.5		
Total	35.1	Total	35.1

[a] Includes loans to security dealers.

Source: Statement by George W. Mitchell, Vice-Chairman, Board of Governors of the Federal Reserve System before the Subcommittee on International Finance of the Committee on Banking, Housing and Urban Affairs, United States Senate, 23 January 1974.

or non-U.S. affiliates of the parent bank. Funds obtained in the U.S. are derived largely from deposits from nonbanks ($5 billion or 16 per cent of total funds), and borrowings from U.S. banks ($6.8 billion or 19 per cent of funds). The data in Table 3-1 indicate that in 1973 foreign banking offices in the U.S. were providing $5 billion more funds than they were obtaining from deposit and other sources of funds in the United States.

The extent of this net contribution of funds to the U.S. economy by foreign banks is a function of relative interest rates and money market pressures in the U.S. and abroad.

Foreign banks employ over a third of their funds to make commercial and industrial loans in the United States, and another ten per cent of their funds in business loans to companies outside the U.S. In addition, they make loans to U.S. and foreign banks, U.S. securities dealers, and invest in money market securities, including U.S. government securities.

D. GROWTH OF OPERATIONS

The volume of foreign bank operations in the United States has grown more rapidly than domestic bank activities. Consequently, the share of foreign banks in credit market activities in the U.S. has tended to increase. This trend is in conformity with global developments where internationally oriented banks (including American banks) have expanded their share of the market.

1. EXPANSION IN NEW YORK

The principal activities of foreign banks with offices in New York are the financing of foreign trade, investment of dollar resources in the U.S. money market, and commercial lending. To a somewhat lesser extent foreign banks have developed a retail banking business, provide portfolio management services for overseas investors, and engage in a broad range of banking services for foreign and domestic customers. A traditional role of foreign banks has been in foreign exchange and foreign remittances.

The asset growth of foreign banks operating from a New York base has been impressive (Table 3-2). In the period 1950–60 assets of foreign banks increased fourfold, and in the subsequent decade enjoyed nearly the same rate of expansion. The growth of foreign-owned subsidiary banks has not been nearly as impressive as that of branches and agencies, in part because the subsidiary banks depend on deposit expansion for their growth. Comparisons of growth between branches and agencies must be initiated around 1965, since the first branches of foreign banks were established in New York in 1961 after enabling legislation was passed in the previous year. In the period

1961–65 a number of agencies were converted to branches, and the resulting statistical biases are impossible to untangle. In the

Table 3-2

Growth of Assets held by Foreign Banks in New York
1950–73

Millions of dollars

	Subsidiary Banks and Trust Companies		New York Branches of Foreign Banks		New York Agencies of Foreign Banks		Total Assets of Foreign Banks
	No.	$	No.	$	No.	$	$
1950	4	82	—	—	24	676	758
1960	9	209	8	244[a]	31	2,774	3,427[a]
1965	10	483	22	1,030	25[b]	3,643	5,156
1972	12	3,408	44	5,349	31	11,536	20,293
1973	12	4,362	46	6,468	33	14,564	25,394

[a] Data for branches refers to 1961, the first year branches of foreign banks were authorised in New York.
[b] The decline between 1960–65 is accounted for by the conversion of some foreign bank agencies to branches after passage of legislation in 1960 authorising foreign banks to operate branches in New York.

Sources: New York State Banking Department; Board of Governors of the Federal Reserve System.

period 1965–73 agency growth has been larger in dollar amount, but at a somewhat lower percentage rate than that of branches. In 1965 agencies accounted for three-fourths of foreign bank assets in New York, and in 1973 they held two-thirds of these assets (Table 3-2).

Subsidiary Banks

Subsidiary banks are varied in their character and operations. At least two basic reasons exist for establishing a subsidiary bank in New York. These are to engage in general banking activities or to perform trust activities which complement the activities of agencies. In the period 1965–1973 the assets of subsidiary banks and trust companies increased nine-fold.

The Canadian chartered banks operate several trust company affiliates in New York which engage mainly in corporate trust operations. This includes performing paying agent functions for their parent banks, partly in connection with Canadian securities sold to American investors. The Canadian trust companies hold a small amount of deposits which are incidental to their trust activities. In 1973 their assets represented approximately 5 per cent of the total held by all foreign bank subsidiaries in New York (Table 3-2).

As of early 1974 the largest foreign owned bank in New York was the Bank of Tokyo Trust Co., an affiliate of the Bank of Tokyo Ltd. and the Industrial Bank of Japan. Organised in 1955, this institution engages in international activities and general banking. With several New York branches and a London branch office, the Bank of Tokyo Trust has grown to rank among the 100 largest banks in the United States. The acquisition of the Franklin National Bank by European-American Bank & Trust in 1974 resulted in that institution becoming the largest foreign owned bank in New York.

Agencies

New York agencies of foreign banks play a prominent role in financing international trade and in the money market. At 31 December 1973 the thirty-three agencies of foreign banks in New York held over $14.5 billion in assets, of which 56 per cent was in loans, 15 per cent funds due from head offices and branches, 14 per cent cash and balances with other banks, 8 per cent claims on customers relative to acceptance financing, and 5 per cent in securities investments. The Canadian and Japanese agencies account for a dominant part of the resources in New York agencies.

The Canadian agencies account for approximately one-fourth of total agency assets in New York. In the 1950s much of their growth stemmed from money market activities in New York. More recently their operations have grown around the expansion of the Canadian banks' international money market and wholesale foreign currency operations. These activities involve the acquisition of U.S. dollars from (1) U.S. corporations and banks, (2) Canadian residents who place U.S.

dollar deposits on a swap basis, (3) Eurodollar deposits, (4) customers serviced by branches and affiliates in the Caribbean and Latin America, (5) sale of Canadian province and municipal bonds in the New York bond market, (6) and settlements of Canadian–U.S. trade balances. Due to the fact that Canada severely restricts American bank solicitation of business at home, the agencies enjoy a substantial advantage in handling the Canadian side of the transaction. With their New York agencies the Canadian banks are able to compete successfully for handling the U.S. side of the transaction as well. In recent years the Canadian agencies in New York have expanded their commercial loans and increased their arbitrage activities between the Eurodollar market and overnight federal funds market.

The Japanese agencies have enjoyed outstanding growth, and by 1972 held over half of the resources of New York agencies. The New York agencies are heavily committed in financing Japanese trade with the United States. However, they provide numerous service functions for their head offices including purchase of export and import bills, dealing in foreign exchange, opening letters of credit, and creating bankers acceptances. The agencies service the large Japanese trading companies which includes providing substantial loan facilities. The funds for these credits have come in part from head offices which in turn have obtained acceptance credits from large American banks. In addition head offices of Japanese banks obtain dollar funds from the Bank of Japan and the Eurodollar market. In addition to head office funds the New York agencies have obtained funds by selling their own acceptances in the U.S., obtained advances from American banks, borrowed directly in the Eurodollar market, and obtained funds in the term federal funds market.

In the three-year period 1970–73 the sources of funds of New York agencies changed considerably. Head offices and branches declined in relative importance as sources of funds. This reflects the currency uncertainties that developed since 1971 and the more cautious attitude of head offices regarding the assumption of an increased dollar exposure position. Second, liabilities for borrowed money became the most important other source of funds, reflecting a more aggressive attitude in agency liability management. Third, funds due to customers and other banks grew in importance. These credit balances ordinarily result from the purchase of a bill of exchange from a customer, from collection of bills of exchange, from sale of customers' securities, by placement of funds with the agency to pay a customer's maturing obligation, or result from creation of margin or cash collateral accounts for letters of credit issued for a customer's account. Between 1970 and 1973 acceptances outstanding increased by nearly $300 million, but accounted for approximately the same proportion of funds as before. New York agencies derive a considerable 'float' advantage from their dollar payments and settlements activities. In 1973 it was reported that the daily volume of transfers involving foreign accounts in U.S. banks exceeded $30 billion. The New York office of a foreign bank can benefit from the float arising out of the time difference between the day its head office sells dollars against local currency to its domestic client and the day the official check is presented in New York by the payee's bank.

Branches

All of the New York branches of foreign banks have been established since 1961 when enabling legislation came into effect. The major activities of these branches are financing foreign trade, commercial loan and deposit, investment of dollar resources for the parent bank organisation, and personal loan and deposit. In the past nearly all of these branches have depended on their trade financing activities for a large portion of the business volume and profitability. In many cases the trade financing involves the U.S. and third country trade, as contrasted with U.S. and home country trade.

The rapid growth of world trade, and the central role of the United States in this trade have provided an expanding base of operations for branches of foreign banks. These branches generally offer a complete range of trade financing services including issue of letters of credit, acceptances, collections, foreign exchange transfers of funds, and remittances. Most of these foreign banks with New York branches have global organisations and provide information concerning the credit status of important customers, government regulations, and tax laws.

In the period 1970–73 the New York branches enjoyed a

substantial growth in resources (180 per cent in the three-year period). This growth was based on their ability to attract a significantly higher volume of deposits in the local banking market, increased liabilities for borrowed money (in the money market), and an increase in funds advanced from head offices and other branches of the parent bank. In recent years these New York branches have bid more aggressively for federal funds, and offered more generous returns on CDs. In the period 1970–73 the use of acceptances as a source of funds actually declined in amount. Foreign deposits (from foreign governments, central banks, and foreign banks) increased at about the same rate as total resources.

2. EXPANSION IN CALIFORNIA

The growth of foreign banking in California is of somewhat more recent vintage than in New York. In addition, there are a number of structural and operational differences that are important. While the bulk of foreign bank resources in New York is housed in the agencies and branches, in California the foreign-owned bank subsidiaries share equal importance with the agencies of foreign banks. In part this results from another difference, namely that while New York permits the licensing of deposit-receiving branches, California only permits agencies (branches would be permitted if FDIC insurance was available on domestic source deposits). California agencies may accept foreign source deposits, though federal law does not permit FDIC insurance of these deposits. Finally, the mix of business of foreign banks in California is somewhat different from that in New York. The subsidiary banking corporations in California have a heavier mixture of retail and consumer type business. Moreover, the foreign banks in California are not closely involved in servicing securities market transactions, investment management, and securities brokerage.

Subsidiary Banks

At yearend 1973 there were eleven state chartered subsidiaries of foreign banks. These subsidiaries operated 113 banking offices throughout 13 of California's 58 counties. Between 1969 and 1973 the deposits in state chartered subsidiaries of foreign banks expanded from $861 million to $2,197 million.

The California subsidiaries clearly perform services aimed at the consumer, and tend to have offices located in the more rapidly growing and densely populated sectors of the state.

Table 3-3

State Chartered Subsidiaries of Foreign Banks as Percentage of Industry in California

	Offices of Subsidiaries as Percentage of Total Offices in State	Deposits in Subsidiaries as Percentage of Total Deposits in State
1960 (Five Banks)	0.63	0.68
1970 (Seven Banks)	2.18	1.46
1971 (Seven Banks)	2.31	2.22
1972 (Eleven Banks)	2.73	2.84
1973 (Eleven Banks)	2.96	3.18

Source: Superintendent of Banks, State of California, *Report on Foreign Banking Matters*, April 1974, p. 32.

The state chartered subsidiaries of foreign banks have increased their share of banking offices and domestic deposits, as is indicated in Table 3-3. These subsidiaries were established initially to service international trade, and in the case of the Japanese-owned subsidiaries in particular to service foreign trade between the United States and Japan. The California subsidiaries assist foreign traders to find customers for their products, provide letters of credit, and purchase and collect bills of exchange. Japan is California's chief trading partner, and the Bank of Tokyo Group which operates a California subsidiary (Bank of Tokyo of California) and agency finances a third of the trade between California and Japan. The subsidiaries also assist foreign business investors (U.S. business firms making outward investments and foreign business firms making investments in the U.S.).[2]

Foreign owned bank subsidiaries in California have competed vigorously for retail business, and a significant portion of their deposits falls into the retail category. Competition has taken the form of offering lower cost checking accounts, and lower interest automobile loans. It could be argued that in a number of cases the California subsidiaries of foreign banks added to the competitiveness of banking to the benefit of the consumer.

Table 3-4

State Chartered Subsidiaries of Foreign Banks, Domestic Deposits, Rank, and Percentage of State Deposits

Calif. Rank	Subsidiary and Year Established	Parent's Country	Domestic Deposits ($ Million)	Percentage of State Total
9	Bank of Tokyo of Calif. (1952)	Japan	731.2	1.03
11	Sumitomo Bank of Calif. (1952)	Japan	570.1	0.80
17	Barclays Bank of Calif. (1965)	Gr. Brit.	229.1	0.32
21	Calif. Canadian Bank (1929)	Canada	171.5	0.24
29	Sanwa Bank of Calif. (1971)	Japan	120.0	0.17
34	Hongkong Bank of Calif. (1955)	Hong Kong	107.3	0.15
39	Bank of Montreal (1918)	Canada	91.3	0.13
44	Mitsubishi Bank of Calif. (1971)		78.7	0.11
52	Chartered Bank of London (1964)	Gr. Brit.	52.9	0.07
93	French Bank of Calif. (1970)	France	22.6	0.03
95	Toronto Dominion Bank of Calif. (1971)	Canada	22.3	0.03
Total Deposits			2,197.5	3.10

Source: Same as in Table 3.3.

Table 3-4 reflects the size of the eleven foreign owned California banks at yearend 1973 in comparison with total deposits in all banks in that state. It should be noted that the four Japanese banks held 2.12 per cent of California deposits, compared with 0.40 per cent for three Canadian banks, and 0.40 per cent for the two British banks. The data in Table 3-4 excludes the deposits of First Western Bank and Trust Co., which was acquired by Lloyds Bank Ltd. in January 1974, and which held close to $1.1 billion in deposits at that time.[3] First Western operated 96 offices at the time of its acquisition.

Agencies

In 1973 there were 28 agencies of foreign banks operating in California. In the period 1969–73 the California agencies increased their assets fourfold, and held over $3 billion in resources at the end of this period. The California agencies do not operate on as broad a basis as the New York agencies. Their balance sheet figures reflect no securities investment holdings, indicating that these functions are concentrated in the New York agencies. Moreover, the California agencies appear to be less dependent on parent bank head offices for funding. Slightly over half of agency funds are derived from borrowed money, and only 9 per cent from foreign deposits.

The California agencies provide credit to correspondent or affiliated banks. Most of the agencies report significant loan participations and commercial lending, and a third indicate that their foreign exchange operation is an important activity. The principal categories of loan customers serviced by California agencies include American banks and corporations engaged in foreign trade financing, American subsidiaries of home country corporations, and foreign subsidiaries of U.S. corporations. The agency form has been elected for use by the Japanese banks in California due to the need to service the heavy borrowing requirements of large Japanese trading companies. The agencies are permitted to lend to individual trading firms amounts in excess of 10 per cent of parent bank capital. By comparison, the lending limits imposed on branches or subsidiaries in the U.S. would represent a burdensome restriction.

4 National Representation Strategies

> A round man cannot be expected to fit
> in a square hole right away.
> He must have time to modify his shape.
>
> Mark Twain

Foreign banks have made use of several basic organisational structures to achieve maximum expansion of the U.S. side of their activities. In the first section of this chapter we examine the organisational structures employed, and in the second we review the strategy approaches developed by foreign banks. The final section of this chapter analyses the prospects for foreign bank expansion in the U.S. during the 1970s.

A. ORGANISATIONAL STRUCTURE

In establishing and expanding their activities in the United States foreign banks have made use of the representative office, the agency, the branch, and the bank subsidiary. Moreover, foreign banks have fallen under the regulatory mantle of the Bank Holding Company Act, and a number of foreign banks (or their affiliates) are technically classified as bank holding companies.[1]

The representative office is the simplest and least expensive organisational form employed by foreign banks. Only one state (California) requires the licensing of representatives of foreign banks, and in this case the formality of licensing is not regarded as burdensome. The functions of a representative do not extend to the conduct of a banking business, but include the promotion of good relations between the foreign bank and the local banking community and business firms which are or may become clients of the parent bank. This might include publicising the name of the parent bank and the nature of services provided by it, developing correspondent banking links, providing for exchange of business information, providing advice concerning local investment opportunities, and appraising the business and regulatory climate in the U.S. Representative offices are regarded as a relatively low cost form of representation. A California survey indicated that in 1973 fourteen representatives of foreign banks had operating budgets averaging $98,200 per office. There were 129 representative offices of foreign banks in the U.S. in 1973.

Two basic disadvantages of the representative office are that it cannot accept deposits, and cannot initiate loans for the parent bank. The agency operation avoids the second of these difficulties.

The term agency refers to a branch office of a foreign bank prohibited by law from accepting deposit accounts. The California Financial Code permits the acceptance of offshore deposits by agencies of foreign banks, and also provides for acceptance of domestic deposits subject to the requirement that FDIC insurance be available. Agencies may incur credit balance liabilities, due to customers and incurred in the ordinary conduct of agency business.

Generally agencies carry out all the functions of representative offices, and in addition have full lending authority. Their authorised lending limit is related to the parent bank's capital accounts. In addition to their lending activities, agencies participate in the foreign exchange market as buyers and sellers; purchase, discount and collect drafts; create acceptances; engage in money market transactions; make payments and transmit funds for their parent banks; and effect interest payments on home country bonds outstanding and held by U.S. investors. Agency operations are flexible, and the agency form enjoys considerable advantages. Reserve requirements and FDIC insurance costs are avoided, but at the cost of sacrificing deposit generating sources of funds. In the past agencies have relied on three sources of funds, including advances of funds from head offices overseas, money market borrowing, and credit balances which are a function of the float (clearing and collection of drafts and cash items).

A branch affords a foreign bank maximum flexibility and opportunity to develop a complete banking business in the United

States. The branch form is used by foreign banks that require a deposit receiving office in the United States, and where this need overcomes the costs relating to reserve requirements.

The Swiss and German banks have used New York branches which complement their U.S. securities affiliate activities. Foreign banks developing a retail banking base in the U.S. may rely on the branch—pure bank affiliate combination. Banks that enjoy an ethnic appeal may tap substantial deposit sources of funds by use of the branch (Puerto Rican and Israeli branches). While the branch may incur higher costs (reserve requirements) than the agency, it can more easily generate local sources of funds via deposits.

New York permits operation of either a branch or an agency, but not both. This has resulted in the use of the agency—subsidiary combination by a number of foreign banks. For example, the Japanese banks have employed this combination in the United States, both in New York and California. Therefore, they have concentrated deposit taking activities in state chartered banking affiliates. This has made it possible for agencies to operate in the commercial lending and trade financing areas, fully backed up by the lending power of the parent banking institution. The Canadian banks also have employed this combination. In New York the Canadian agencies emphasise short-term investments in loans to securities brokers and dealers and investments in other liquid assets. The Canadian agencies are backed up by U.S. dollar exchange provided by their head offices in Canada. The extent of this backup is largely a function of alternative investment opportunities in the Eurodollar market, and loan opportunities at home. Domestic loans are then financed by swaps of U.S. dollars into Canadian dollars, which may carry an associated exchange risk. Independently, the Canadian trust companies in New York service the obligations of Canadian borrowers held by U.S. investors, as well as function as corporate trustees. In California the Canadian agencies service loan requirements of corporate customers, and assist in financing foreign trade. The California subsidiaries of Canadian banks conduct an essentially retail oriented business.

In the case of state chartered subsidiaries that conduct a

banking business, the provisions of the Bank Holding Company Act generally become applicable. The 1970 amendment to the Bank Holding Company Act was a landmark in several respects. It provides ground rules that apply to all acquisitions of American banks. Second, it provides for clear and definite jurisdiction by the Board of Governors over national and state banks, and more especially over state non-member as well as state member banks. Third, the 1970 amendment provides for a formal administrative and legal system for holding company acquisitions of U.S. banks, including a 'pre-hearing' and administrative ruling. The Board of Governors renders such rulings, subject to reconsideration based upon submission of further evidence.

A final difference in the 1970 amendment is its application to the non-banking area. Bank holding companies are permitted to acquire nonbank companies in areas of finance considered complementary to commercial banking. The Board of Governors has attempted to specify those areas of finance that banks and BHCs may expand into within certain guidelines.

Foreign banks have found the holding company structure a useful and flexible adjunct as they have developed their activities in the United States. We further consider this organisational approach in subsequent chapters.

B. STRATEGY APPROACHES

A foreign bank may opt for one of several methods of expansion in the United States. Two expansion methods stand out as embodying totally different objectives and combinations of operating units. These are (1) the branch-securities affiliate combination, and (2) the pure-bank-affiliate route which seems to exclude the possibility of retaining or developing an interest in the securities business.

The investment and acquisition strategies of foreign banks tend to reflect the regulatory stance of state and federal authorities in the U.S., as well as the type of banking systems that prevail in the home country. In Switzerland and Germany banks are permitted to engage in a wide range of activities including deposit, loan, underwriting, investment management, and securities trading and brokerage. The large German and Swiss banks are major factors on the stock exchanges in their countries. Several of the large German and Swiss banks have established New York branches, but none of these banks has acquired a controlling interest in an American bank. However, each has established a securities and underwriting affiliate that operates from a New York office. For example, the Swiss Credit Bank owns and operates the Swiss American Corporation, which at yearend 1972 ranked 110th in capital position of U.S. investment banking firms with $8 million of its own capital funds. This firm underwrites and distributes securities and provides investment advisory services. The Union Bank of Switzerland together with the Deutsche Bank formed the UBS-DB Corporation, an investment banking–securities affiliate. At yearend 1972 this firm had equity capital of $7.1 million. Similarly, the Swiss Bank Corporation operates the Basle Securities Corporation, an underwriting and securities affiliate.

The big three German banks tend to parallel the Swiss institutions in their U.S. representation, in that it has been confined largely to investment banking or securities affiliates. In addition, the large German banks have established branch offices in New York. We have already referred to the Deutsche Bank investment in UBS-DB Corporation, New York. In 1970 the CCB Group (Commerzbank, Crédit Lyonnais, and Banco di Roma) formed EuroPartners Securities Corporation, which engages in underwriting and securities brokerage with the bulk of its business involved in servicing foreign investors trading in U.S. securities. At yearend 1972 EuroPartners had an equity capital of $5.8 million and ranked 137th in capital position of U.S. investment banking firms. Early in 1972 four European banks formed ABD Securities Corporation, to conduct a general securities and investment banking business. This firm succeeded the ABN Corporation, previously owned by the Algemene Bank Nederland N.V. and German-American Securities Corporation, formerly owned by the Dresdner Bank A.G. Two new participants, members of the ABECOR group of European banks, Banque de Bruxelles, S.A., Brussels, and Bayerische Hypotheken and Wechselbank, Munich each took 25 per cent participations in the new company. At yearend 1972 the capitalisation of ABD Securities Corporation was $5.6 million.

The large British clearing banks appear to have followed the pure-bank-affiliate route in acquiring interests in U.S. banks. Through its wholly-owned affiliate Barclays Bank International Ltd., Barclays Bank Ltd., London operates several subsidiaries, and direct branches in Chicago and Boston. Barclays Bank of California operates 23 branches in California. In addition the London parent institution operates Barclays Bank of New York, which was organised in 1971 by conversion of the parent bank's branch in New York City. In 1974 the New York subsidiary of Barclays acquired the First Westchester National Bank, a 19-office institution holding $220 million in assets. Early in 1973 the New York State Banking Department had rejected Barclays application to acquire the $431 million Long Island Trust Co., Garden City, New York, due to possible adverse effects on competition in the New York–Long Island banking market (see Appendix B for summary).

The expansion of Barclays in the United States on an interstate basis poses difficult questions for U.S. regulatory authorities since domestic banks are not permitted to operate banking offices in more than one state. Therefore, foreign banks such as Barclays can be considered to hold a competitive advantage over domestic banks in this important area. A number of considerations prompt non-U.S. banks such as Barclays to remain optimistic regarding the regulatory treatment of their expanding U.S. representation. First, a number of foreign banks similarly operate across state lines, including several large Canadian and Japanese banks. These include the Bank of Montreal, Canadian Imperial Bank of Commerce, and the Bank of Tokyo Ltd. Second, a growing number of U.S. banks operate on a multi-state basis without the use of deposit accepting offices. This includes establishment of separate Edge Act international banking affiliates (which accept international deposits) in principal centres such as New York, San Francisco, Chicago, Los Angeles, Miami, New Orleans, and Houston. In addition, major U.S. banks are establishing or planning to establish near-banking or quasi-banking offices across state lines, representing consumer finance, loan servicing, data processing, and commercial financing activities via affiliate institutions.[2] Third, U.S. banks are pressing regulatory authorities to allow interstate operations.

A second large British institution, Lloyds Bank Ltd., consummated the purchase of First Western Bank and Trust Co., Los Angeles from World Airways Inc. for a reported $115 million. This took effect in January 1974. Announcement of this acquisition proposal was made in June 1973, shortly after the New York Superintendent of Banks had denied the request of Barclays to acquire the Long Island Trust Co. Both the Board of Governors of the Federal Reserve and the California State Superintendent approved the acquisition in December 1973. Prior to this Lloyds had announced its intention to add $10 million in capital to First Western, to reduce dividend payments so as to further strengthen the new affiliates equity position, and to rebuild First Western's management which had suffered from high turnover due to uncertainties concerning ultimate ownership status. The Board of Governors indicated it would later rule on Lloyds' request to retain indirect investment in several financing and export credit subsidiaries.

In 1973 foreign bankers had awaited the decision of state and federal regulatory authorities with some concern. Rejection of the proposal to acquire First Western would have reinforced suspicions that the U.S. was following a protectionist policy, and could have had an adverse effect on foreign government attitudes toward American banks operating overseas. Alternately, approval of the Lloyds acquisition of First Western could result in further proposals for tighter control of foreign bank operations in the United States. In 1973 Representative Wright Patman had already submitted a federal licensing bill to Congress, and the Federal Reserve had a study in process concerning the activities of foreign banks in the U.S.

The acquisition of First Western by Lloyds was an extremely important step, due to the size of the California bank (ranked eighth in California and 66th nationally), the size of Lloyds in world rankings (ranked 28th among free world banks in the 1972 American Banker survey), and the growing proportionate influence of foreign banks in the state of California. It appears that in recent years the British banks have been placing greater emphasis on development of a retail banking base in the U.S. In part this may be viewed as a trend necessitated by the loss of significant operating bases in Asia and Africa, resulting from nationalisation and pressures for substantial home ownership of banks in these countries.

The Canadian banks also have developed a sizeable retail banking business in the United States, primarily in California. Their New York representation has focused on agency money market operations and corporate trust activities. In 1973 a large Canadian trust company, Royal Trust of Montreal, acquired the Inter-National Bank of Miami, Florida. This acquisition was completed with Federal Reserve Board approval under the Bank Holding Company Act, despite objections of Florida authorities. In 1972 Royal Trust of Montreal had assets of Cdn. $2.1 billion and managed trust assets of Cdn. $10.5 billion. Royal Trust is the largest mortgage company in Canada, the largest real estate company, and manages a mutual fund. The Miami acquisition fits into a broad expansion plan that the Canadian parent bank made public in 1973, including development of trust and estate planning services in Florida using Inter-National as a base of operations. In the past Royal Trust has grown through acquisition rather than from establishing banks *de novo*.

The Japanese banks also have employed the pure bank affiliate route successfully in California. However, they have used it in combination with large doses of non-retail oriented operating units. For example, New York State chartered affiliates pursue a wholesale and internationally oriented banking business. Finally, the agencies of Japanese banks in the United States tend to complement head office activities in the U.S., through their loans to large home country trading firms, financing of foreign trade, and management of short-term dollar assets and liabilities.

As noted at the beginning of this section, foreign banks represented in the U.S. have developed organisational frameworks that best service the parent banks requirements, and these needs in turn are related to the style of banking pursued in the home country. The British banks have pursued an extensive branch system to develop a broad retail base. The Swiss and German banks have geared U.S. representation toward servicing the securities and investment needs of their customers. This tends to back up home country operations on the stock exchanges and new issues markets. The Canadian banks have a retail base in California, a money market operation in New

York, and corporate trust services in New York. The corporate trust activity relates to servicing the extensive borrowing undertaken by Canadian governments and utilities in the U.S. The money market activity tends to round out the global foreign exchange and money management operations of the Canadian banks, which are extensive and well developed considering the size of the Canadian economy and financial system. Finally, the Japanese banks have developed U.S. representation that blends retail, dollar sourcing, corporate lending, trade financing, and funds management. All of these functions complement and complete the global needs of the Japanese banks and the Japanese economy.

C. CHANGING STRATEGIES IN THE 1970s

The pace and form of expansion of foreign banking in the United States during the current decade will be influenced by several variables. Prominent among these will be the global environment for international banking, changing patterns and trends in American banking, and the regulatory environment in the U.S.

Thus far in the 1970s the environment for international banking has been influenced by new developments including the removal of the U.S. capital controls programme early in 1974, and the oil energy crisis which has placed heavy balance of payments pressures on the petroleum importing countries. Removal of capital controls by the U.S. authorities came at a strategic time, considering the important role that American financial markets could play in intermediating 'petrodollars' accumulated by petroleum exporting nations. Only a few financial mechanisms are available through which the additional foreign exchange earned by petroleum exporting nations can be recycled, so as to avoid placing extreme payments pressures on oil importers.

The dynamics of American banking probably will make it an important growth industry for many years to come. The only question is, in a global context will American banking continue to rank as a more attractive growth vehicle than the majority of world industry sectors? Recent trends suggest that this question should be answered in the affirmative for the balance of the current decade. Innovative American banks have been finding new outlets for expansion through the bank holding company structure, and their competitors in the industry have been quick to follow. In the following chapter we examine the changing structure of American banking in more detail, and consider the role of foreign banks in accelerating this change.

The regulatory framework in the U.S. may be modified somewhat, as it applies to foreign banks. In this connection it is possible that additional constraints may be imposed on the organisational choices open to foreign banks, as well as on the scope of their operations in the United States. This area is discussed in Chapter 7.

To summarise, for the balance of this decade it is probable that foreign banks will adapt their organisational strategies to the changing environment they face globally and in the United States. This process of adaptation will have to cope with new opportunities to compete for business in a dynamically changing American banking market, and may require that foreign banks address themselves to a more restrictive regulatory posture in the U.S. To compete for petrodollars and other types of loanable funds, foreign banks may have to develop new financial intermediary packages in attempting to attract dollar funds channelled through the U.S. financial markets. In addition, outside the U.S. foreign banks will have to develop a stronger competitive thrust in the Eurodollar and other financial market sectors. In both instances foreign banks may have to ally themselves with local institutions in the form of consortium banking institutions or less formal group structures.

II
IMPACT OF FOREIGN BANKING AND INVESTMENT ON U.S.

5 Impact on U.S. Banking and Finance

> Before I built a wall I'd ask to know
> what I was walling in or walling out.
>
> Robert Frost

A. TRENDS IN BANKING STRUCTURE

The banking structure in the United States is unique in many respects. The primary jurisdiction of each of the fifty states has yielded fifty different state banking systems, each with its own rules on branching, ease of entry for new banking entities, and degree of monopolistic concentration. At one extreme stand New York and California with highly competitive banking market structures. At the opposite extreme are a number of states which do not permit any branch banking and in which exist pockets of geographically separated non-competing banking markets. This latter category of state banking system generally does not permit foreign banking corporations to operate within its borders and does not permit control of state banks by foreign shareholders.

The expansion of foreign banks into the U.S. credit markets has more than doubled the number of big banks operating within the United States that refuse to recognise territorial limits or regional constraints. This substantial admixture of large competitive banking units has resulted in the following changes in operating policies and regulatory philosophy:

1. Large U.S. banks have sought to increase their efficiency and ability to respond competitively. This is evidenced by the formation of out of state Edge Act affiliates by a number of large banking institutions and in some cases by the conversion from state to national charter (e.g. the First Pennsylvania Banking & Trust

Company application in 1974).

2 Medium size U.S. banks have endeavoured to strengthen themselves by formation of Bank Holding Company units in states that limit or prohibit branch banking. In this way larger banking units have been organised in a number of important states such as Florida, New Jersey, and Minnesota.

3 Regulatory authorities in several states have attempted to modify their approach toward supervision and control of domestic banking units so as to give them the opportunity to respond to a more competitive banking environment.

4 Regulatory authorities in some states have endeavoured to limit access of foreign banks to their credit markets by imposing ownership restrictions on bank shares.

5 Federal regulatory authorities have permitted expansion of across-state activities via bank holding companies, within operational areas considered to be reasonable.

6 A number of large U.S. banks have formulated plans that would easily accommodate a transition to a system of nationwide banking operations.

Since the early 1960s American banking has become more dynamic and innovative. In the past decade American banks have seized upon opportunities to rationalise their organisational structures so as better to service customers and extend the market area. In this connection at least five structural changes appear to stand out in importance in the commercial banking field. These include the development of widening differences between large and small banks, increased use of the bank holding company as a means of effecting innovation, the appearance of wider branching privileges within a larger number of states, expanded scope for interstate representation, and extension of banks into near banking and related fields of endeavour.

Differences between large and small banks have sharpened. Large banks have been growing faster, have introduced a wide variety of new services, and have been more aggressive and flexible in adopting growth strategies. By contrast, small banks have not been able to maintain the same marketing strategy where offering new services is concerned. These differences between large and small banks have been amplified by the growing presence of foreign banking institutions in the United States. Only the large American banks are in a position to do business with and provide the broad range of services called for by foreign banks. Only the large American banks are able to effectively compete with foreign banks in U.S. banking markets.

The bank holding company represents one of the most important and dynamic aspects of American banking structure. At yearend 1972 some 1,607 bank holding companies controlled 2,720 American banks with assets of over $467 billion. This represented close to 20 per cent of American banks and over 63 per cent of American bank assets.

Twenty of the fifty states in the U.S. permit holding companies to acquire bank stocks, and several additional states permit such acquisitions with approval of the state authorities. The remaining states impose a variety of restrictions on bank holding companies including limits on the proportion of deposits in the state held by any single holding company, and restrictions on multibank holding company operations. It has been noted that multibank holding companies have spread rapidly in several unit banking states such as Florida and Minnesotta, and bank holding company group expansion has substituted for branching.[1]

Foreign banks operating in the U.S. have made effective use of the bank holding company form of organisation. The holding company structure has made it possible for foreign banks to adopt more flexible strategies in expanding their financing and related operations in the United States, adding to competitive pressures and the need for American banks themselves to find new avenues of dynamic response.

Commercial banks have sought and obtained wider branching privileges. During the 1960s several states, including Maine, New Hampshire, New Jersey, New York, and Wisconsin, moved in the direction of permitting more liberal branching by banks operating within their borders. In 1969 New Jersey enacted a law which divided the state into three districts. Banks are permitted to merge and establish branches within these districts. Moreover, state-wide holding companies are permitted under this legislation, subject to a limitation on the proportion of bank deposits that can be held by any one holding company group. In 1975 the Florida legislature passed a county-wide branching law. In general there appears to be a slow but inexorable tendency toward granting the branching privilege, and extending this privilege across a wider area within each state.

Foreign banks have been keenly interested in the extension of wider branching privileges, especially in important international banking states such as New York, Illinois, and Pennsylvania (California already permits state-wide branching). In some cases both foreign and U.S. banks enjoy a community of interest in any possible liberalisation of state laws regarding bank branching. This has been the case especially in unit banking states where no provision exists for licensing branches of foreign banks. In 1973 Illinois enacted a law permitting the licensing of branches of foreign banks in the Chicago Loop district. However, there is still a bitter debate concerning the possible extension of branching privileges to domestic banks in Illinois.

The fifty states have jealously guarded the bank chartering and licensing prerogative within their own borders. Despite this, numerous exceptions exist to the prohibition on interstate banking, and new pressures are steadily mounting to break down this barrier against a wider base of geographic operations. The major exceptions thus far include the following:

1. grandfather protection in the case of Bank of California branches in Oregon and Washington;
2. banking activities of bank holding companies (Northwest Bancorporation operates 79 banks in Minnesota, Montana, Wisconsin and several additional states, and Western Bancorporation operates 23 banks in Arizona, California, Colorado and several additional states);
3. Edge Act affiliates of U.S. banks conducting international banking operations in banking centres in other states;
4. representative offices of major banks located in other states;
5. near banking activities of bank holding companies;

6 foreign bank holding companies with branches, affiliates and agencies in several states.

The near banking activities of bank holding companies that have been approved by the Board of Governors include the following: dealer in bankers acceptances, mortgage company activities, operation of a finance company, operation of a credit card affiliate, factoring, industrial banking, servicing loans, trust company activities, investment adviser to real estate investment trusts and investment companies under the Investment Company Act of 1940, providing general economic advice and information, providing advice on portfolio management, leasing, investment in community welfare projects, data processing and book-keeping services, insurance agent or broker in credit extension, underwriting credit life insurance, and providing armoured car and courier services.[2]

Foreign bank holding companies represent a comparatively new factor in the area of interstate operations. However, the extension of their interstate activities has focused renewed interest on the possibilities of removing or at least modifying the prohibition against interstate banking operations. The most significant examples of interstate banking by foreign owned institutions are confined to banks of three countries, Great Britain, Japan, and Canada.

At present Barclays Bank Ltd. has the largest representation in the U.S. of any of the British banks. Barclays operates three branches in New York via its affiliate Barclays Bank International Ltd., and operates a New York State chartered affiliate Barclays Bank of New York. In 1973 regulatory authorities approved the merger of the $168 million First Westchester Bank into Barclays Bank of New York. In addition Barclays operates a state chartered affiliate in California, Barclays Bank of California, San Francisco. Early in 1974 Barclays indicated its intent to merge the County Bank, Santa Barbara with Barclays Bank of California which was approved by state and federal regulatory authorities. Barclays also operates branch offices in Chicago and Boston.

The Bank of Tokyo Ltd. also operates on an interstate basis in the United States. Its representation includes substantial ownership in a New York affiliate, the Bank of Tokyo Trust,[3] ownership of a California affiliate, Bank of Tokyo of California; joint ownership of a Chicago affiliate; a Chicago branch; and a New York agency.

B. HOW FOREIGN BANKS INFLUENCE STRUCTURE

There are three important avenues through which foreign banks may influence U.S. banking structure. These include (1) competition for bank loans and deposits, (2) operating over a wider geographic base, and (3) participating in the securities and investment banking fields. In the following sections we discuss the first two avenues. Discussion of the activities of foreign banks in the securities—investment banking fields is reserved for Chapter 6.

1. COMPETITION FOR BANK LOANS AND DEPOSITS

It is an accepted fact that foreign banks have become important loan participants in the U.S. credit markets. This is attested to in the tombstone prospectuses and other notices encountered in the *Wall Street Journal* and other financial publications describing bank loan syndicate placements. This participation is reflected in the closer alignment between Eurodollar lending rates and the U.S. prime rate. Finally, the importance of foreign bank participation in the U.S. loan markets is reflected by the concern of Federal Reserve authorities over the possible extent of neutralisation of domestic monetary policy that results from inflows of offshore funds, in part faciliated by the U.S. agencies and branches of European, Canadian and other non-U.S. institutions.[4] Foreign banks not enjoying direct representation in the United States have participated in such loans to U.S. companies, and it has been estimated that offshore funds and funds provided by U.S. agencies and branches of foreign banks represent eight per cent or more of bank credits to U.S. domestic corporations.[5] Removal of the foreign investment and lending restraints by the U.S. government and Federal Reserve Board early in 1974 should accelerate the tendency already apparent for the U.S. and Eurodollar markets to drift closer together.[6]

Potential Deposit Competition
Competition for bank deposits requires direct representation, and is present in those several states in which foreign banks

enjoy branch, agency and affiliate facilities. Foreign bank activity is a significant part of the total in two states only (New York and California). In all other states foreign bank competition for deposit funds cannot be considered highly significant. However, it is important to recognise the existence of potential competition in the market for deposit funds. What part of the deposit structure in American banks potentially could be bid for by foreign owned banking institutions, or by foreign bank branches? Which banks hold a high proportion of deposits that could be subject to competition from foreign banks? Would a significant proportion of deposits residing in the large banks in each state represent an area of such potential competition?

Bank deposit structure varies considerably from state to state, reflecting local wealth and income patterns, size and number of banks, branching regulations, and mix of local and regional business. In a previous study this author pointed out that the 200 largest banking institutions in the U.S. account for the bulk of international banking operations,[7] and probably hold the bulk if not all of the corporate deposits in American banks subject to international competitive pressures. In the following analysis we estimate the proportion of commercial bank deposits in each state subject to potential international competition to obtain approximate orders of magnitude for comparison on a state-by-state basis.[8]

In Table 5-1 we have isolated the 172 largest banks in the United States, which includes all commercial banks with deposits of $500 million or more.[9] These banks hold over 48 per cent of bank deposits in the United States, and include virtually all of the international banking resources in the American banking system. Column 2 of Table 5-1 indicates the number of large banks per state and Column 4 reflects the proportion of bank deposits in that state held by large banks, i.e. exposed to potential international competition.

The overall results of Table 5-1 are summarised in Table 5-2 (see p. 55).

In four states (California, New York, Rhode Island, and Arizona) 80 per cent or more of total deposits reside in banks subject to international competition. These include the two major international banking and foreign bank representation states in the U.S., namely California and New York. In five states

Table 5-1
Deposits in Commercial Banks Facing Potential Competition from Foreign Banks, by State
31 December 1973

State or Area	Total Number of Banks	Number of Banks Exposed to International Competition	Deposits in Banks Exposed to International Competition $ Million	Percentage of State or Area Total
	1	2	3	4
United States	14,194	172	333,548	48.7
Alabama	287	1	880	1.1
Alaska	10	—	—	—
Arizona	22	3	4,650	80.4
Arkansas	258	—	—	—
California	185	12	63,373	89.5
Colorado	302	2	1,423	21.2
Connecticut	68	3	3,396	49.4
Delaware	19	1	575	32.3
Wash., D.C.	15	2	1,955	57.0
Florida	646	1	1,173	51.4
Georgia	436	4	4,185	37.7
Hawaii	12	2	1,608	68.0
Idaho	24	2	1,379	64.1
Illinois	1,172	7	23,484	45.1
Indiana	410	3	3,194	20.9

Iowa	670	—	—
Kansas	612	—	—
Kentucky	342	2	1,360	17.4
Louisiana	245	2	1,614	16.6
Maine	48	—	—	—
Maryland	112	5	4,507	59.9
Massachusetts	153	4	6,955	49.0
Michigan	340	9	14,143	52.6
Minnesota	740	3	3,307	26.2
Mississippi	181	2	1,237	25.2
Missouri	687	3	2,736	18.2
Montana	151	—	—	—
Nebraska	449	—	—	—
Nevada	8	1	805	46.0
New Hampshire	82	—	—	—
New Jersey	222	8	6,084	29.9
New Mexico	74	—	—	—
New York	304	23	99,144	84.0
North Carolina	90	5	8,061	69.4
North Dakota	170	—	—	—
Ohio	498	13	12,785	45.4
Oklahoma	452	3	1,815	21.9
Oregon	46	2	4,212	76.1
Pennsylvania	422	14	22,709	57.2
Rhode Island	16	2	2,035	82.4
South Carolina	91	1	787	21.2
South Dakota	159	—	—	—
Tennessee	321	5	4,515	38.9
Texas	1,266	9	10,312	26.9
Utah	54	1	747	27.7

State or Area	Total Number of Banks	Number of Banks Exposed to International Competition	Deposits in Banks Exposed to International Competition $ Million	Percentage of State or Area Total
	1	2	3	4
Vermont	39	—	—	—
Virginia	271	4	3,476	28.5
Washington	88	4	5,426	70.5
West Virginia	210	—	—	—
Wisconsin	621	2	1,907	14.7
Wyoming	71	—	—	—

Source: Federal Deposit Insurance Corporation.

(Oregon, Washington, Hawaii, North Carolina, and Idaho) between 60.1 per cent and 80 per cent of deposits reside in banks

Table 5-2

Analysis of Exposure to Potential International Competition, by State, 31 December 1973

Percentage Deposits in Commercial Banks subject to International Competition	Number of States
0– 20	19
20.1– 40	13
40.1– 60	10
60.1– 80	5
80.1–100	4
	51

Source: Table 5.1.

subject to international competition. States that appear to be under-represented include Illinois, Pennsylvania, and Texas. These are states where unit banking (Illinois and Texas) or limited branching (Pennsylvania) restrict the growth of individual banks, and tend to make for a smaller average size of banking institution. It is highly significant to find that a number of states have a fairly high proportion of deposits in their large banking institutions that are subject to potential international competition, suggesting that adoption of more liberal policies by the respective state legislatures toward licensing of foreign banking operations could result in attracting one or more foreign banks to each of these states.

The conclusions are clear. A number of states have a high percentage of deposits in large banks that are subject to potential foreign competition for deposits. On a national basis over 48 per cent of deposits reside in large banks, those exposed to international competition. In short, a number of state banking markets probably would be subject to greater competitive pressures by foreign banks if state legislatures provided for chartering and licensing of foreign banks. The prevailing deposit structure would serve to attract these foreign banking institutions. By excluding foreign banks a number of state banking markets are isolated from potential competition that could contribute materially to the efficiency and financial services in those credit market sectors.

2. WIDER BASE OF OPERATIONS

Foreign banks have been able to expand their U.S. representation on an interstate basis. Of the more than 160 foreign banks with some form of U.S. representation in 1974, 53 enjoyed representation in more than one state.[10]

The interstate operations of foreign banks have affected U.S. banking and credit market structure in at least four ways. First, interest rates in regional credit and banking markets have become more closely aligned. Formerly isolated pockets of high cost loan funds, and low return deposit opportunities have been narrowed down by the competitive inroads of foreign banks, and by the competitive responses of domestic banks. Second, the interstate representation garnered by foreign banks has forced large American banks to reassess their competitive status. As a result, large American banks have sought to respond to the challenge by preparing themselves for interstate operations, and by seeking legislative change that would permit them a wider geographic base of operations. By contrast small American banks have tended to react in a less positive manner, and have tended to support state banking legislation that would restrict the expansion of foreign banks in their states. Finally, regulatory authorities have reacted in a variety of ways to the expansion of interstate operations. At the state level existing prohibitions against foreign bank entry have been reaffirmed.[11]

An interesting example of state banking authority review of the status of foreign bank entry took place in California in 1973–74. A moratorium on processing applications for branches submitted by foreign owned banks was used to give the State Superintendent of Banks an opportunity to carefully review the impact on banking structure of foreign bank expansion in that state. In March 1973 California imposed a moratorium on applications for new branches by state chartered foreign bank subsidiaries. In September, shortly after defeat of proposed restrictive foreign banking legislation in the state senate, the ban was lifted for those applications which had been pending at the time the moratorium was imposed. In December 1973 the California State Banking Department announced it would resume processing applications for branches in downtown San Francisco and downtown Los Angeles. In April 1974 the moratorium was removed for applications in all other areas of the state. In May 1974 it was announced that nearly half of the branch applications submitted by state chartered foreign subsidiary banks and pending during the moratorium period had been denied. While the fifty per cent denial rate exceeded the normal turndown rate of 20 per cent, the incidence of denials was heavier among the larger foreign banks with more substantial representation in California and possessing some interstate representation. Smaller banks seeking local branches enjoyed a higher rate of approvals than larger banks competing on a state-wide and interstate basis.[12] It should be further noted that in this same time period California approved the formation of five state chartered subsidiary banks owned by foreign banking and business groups.[13] In addition, four new foreign bank agencies were approved in the period overlapping that in which the branch denials had taken place.

C. INTERNATIONAL ORIENTATION OF NEW YORK MONEY MARKET

The New York money market is a reservoir of liquid claims in which participants exchange asset and liability relationships so as to increase or diminish their liquidity positions in the short run. Nearly all participant groups conduct a substantial volume of international transactions which ultimately clear through the New York market.

The New York market is characterised by its massive size, the wide range of asset-liability options available, its relative stability, and the extent of international orientation. The international orientation of the New York money market can be reflected by data which measures the dollar value of money market type assets held by non-residents. In Table 5-3 we bring together data that reflect foreign ownership. This table has been assembled with the objective of measuring the size of the money market and its major component parts, reflecting foreign ownership of money market and near substitute assets, and isolating the holdings of official international reserves held by governments and central banks. This indicates the direct and indirect influence of overseas pressures on the market, and in turn the relative burden borne by the market in accomodating the needs of internationally oriented participants and residents of countries other than the United States.

In 1974 official international reserves held in dollar assets invested in the money market and in near substitutes were equivalent to almost twenty-five per cent of the total market. At the same time foreign liquid and short-term assets held in the U.S. represented over thirty-eight per cent of the total market. At yearend 1974 total official international reserves of member countries of the International Monetary Fund were $222 billion, of which the foreign exchange component represented $156.6 billion. Close to half of this foreign exchange component is held in the form of U.S. dollar liabilities to non-residents ($76.2 billion in Table 5-3). In short, the New York money market plays a vital role as depository for official international reserves. The presence of foreign banks in New York enhances and facilitates this role.

While a significant part of the New York money market is absorbed as international reserve holdings of foreign governments and central banks, the market exceeds the global total of international reserves (also held in the form of sterling, gold, SDRs and reserve positions in the IMF). The New York market continues to hold a size advantage over the Eurocurrency market (Table 5-4). Moreover, it enjoys other significant advantages over the Eurocurrency market, which is essentially an interbank market and subject to the vicissitudes of volatility and thinning out in periods of financial crisis. Foreign banks can secure a more stable retail-wholesale deposit base in the United States, and together with timely aggressiveness in related money market sectors (dollar CDs, and federal funds) can operate on a more secure and well-entrenched basis.

The asset holdings of foreign banks in the United States provide an approximate and indirect indication of their potential importance in the New York money market. Naturally, a large part of foreign bank assets in the United States tend to be divorced from money market activities, and are invested in loans to corporate customers and consumers. However, foreign

Foreign Ownership of Money Market Assets in New York 1973–74

(Billions of dollars)

Money Market Assets	Official International Reserves Held in the U.S. 1973	Official International Reserves Held in the U.S. 1974	New York Money Market 1973	New York Money Market 1974	Portion of Money Market Assets held by Non-Residents 1973	Portion of Money Market Assets held by Non-Residents 1974
U.S. Treasury Bills	31.5	34.7	107.8	119.7	31.9	35.2
Commercial Paper			41.1	49.1		
Bankers Acceptances	6.3[a]	10.6[a]	8.9	18.5	18.4[a]	32.6[a]
Large Negotiable CDs			43.7	92.9		
Federal Funds Sold			14.1	20.2		
Loans to Securities Brokers & Dealers			9.2	4.9		
Sub-Total	37.8	45.3	224.8	305.3	50.3	67.8
Substitutes for Money Market Assets						
Marketable & Non-Marketable U.S. Government Securities	21.2	21.3			21.6	21.8
Demand Deposits	2.1	3.0			11.3	14.1
Time Deposits	3.9	4.3			7.1	10.1
Other Assets[b]	1.7	2.2			2.3	3.1
Total	66.8	76.2	224.8	305.3	92.6	116.9
Percentage of Money Market Assets	29.9%	25.0%	100.0%	100.0%	41.3%	38.3%

[a] Also includes commercial paper and negotiable time CDs.
[b] Long-term liabilities reported by U.S. banks and debt securities of U.S. federally sponsored agencies, and amounts payable in foreign currencies.

Source: *Federal Reserve Bulletin*; IMF, *International Financial Statistics*; and U.S. *Treasury Bulletin*.

banks can place considerable pressure on the money market, and especially on narrow sectors of that market including fed-

Table 5-4

Size Comparison of New York Money Market and International Asset Categories 1973–74

	Billions of dollars		Percentage of N.Y. Money Market	
	1973	1974	1973	1974
New York Money Market	224.8	305.3	100.0	100.0
World Official Reserves	184.3	222.0	81.9	72.8
U.S. Liquid and Other Liabilities to Foreigners	92.6	116.9	41.3	38.3
Eurocurrency Market	193.0	227.0	85.8	74.4
Total Assets of Foreign Banks in U.S.	38.0	56.0	16.9	18.3
Total Assets of Foreign Branches of U.S. Banks	79.5	151.5	35.3	49.7

Source: IMF, *International Financial Statistics; Federal Reserve Bulletin;* and Bank of England, *Quarterly Bulletin.*

eral funds and loans to brokers and dealers. Finally, we should note that foreign branches of American banks can exert far more leverage on the money market than foreign banks in the U.S. Foreign branches of U.S. banks hold over two-and-a-half times the resources of foreign banks operating in the United States, enjoy direct links via their head offices, and are in a position to function as important and at times critical sources of Eurodollar reserve adjustment for their parent institutions.

1. SOURCE OF FUNDS

The U.S. credit markets regularly provide considerable loan funds to foreign borrowers. During the period of capital controls (1964–74) when the Interest Equalization Tax (IET) and foreign lending restraint programme limited U.S. bank credits to overseas areas this credit sector grew only slightly. Following removal of these restrictions early in 1974 claims on foreigners reported by banks in the United States accelerated rapidly.[14] At October 1973 banks in the U.S. had outstanding loans and claims on foreigners of $23.9 billion. The larger part of this represented short-term claims, with loans making up nearly $7 billion of total short-term claims. A good portion of short-term loans represent those extended to banks outside the United States. Collections and acceptances made for the purpose of providing dollar funds for foreigners represent important sources for generating credit funds for residents outside the United States.

Foreign banks operating in the U.S. via agencies, branches and state chartered subsidiaries play a highly significant role in providing credits to non-resident borrowers located outside the U.S. Through their U.S. offices foreign banks provide short-term and long-term credits to borrowers outside the United States, and create acceptance credits to service non-U.S. banks and corporate customers. Finally, foreign banks operating through U.S. banking offices process collections against offshore business firms and process payments representing the clearing and ultimate settlement of a variety of transactions.

In Chapter 3 we have seen that at October 1973 foreign banks held claims against banks and others outside the United States which in the aggregate amounted to $8.9 billion (Table 3-1). This represents over one-third of the total claims against foreign banks, business firms and other non-residents held by all banking institutions in the U.S. at the same date. From this we can see that foreign banks play a major role in functioning as a conduit through which funds can be made available to borrowers outside the United States. The preceding should not be interpreted to mean that this role is one-directioned. The same data in Table 3-1 indicate that foreign banks in the U.S. had obtained over $13 billion of funds from outside the United States.

2. DEPOSITORY AND SAFEKEEPING FUNCTION

We touched on the role of New York as an international depository and safekeeper of liquid funds in the opening section of this chapter. There we noted that in 1974 foreign governments and central banks held over $76 billion of official monetary reserves in the form of money market and related types of dollar assets in the U.S. Secondly, at yearend 1974 an additional $38 billion of short-term claims was held by foreign banks and business firms.

Foreign banks accounted for over $29 billion of this amount, and other holders (mainly business firms) held over $8 billion. Nearly $20 billion of foreign bank claims in the U.S. were in the form of money market assets (bankers acceptances, commercial paper and time certificates of deposit), and over $10 billion in deposits. The New York offices of foreign banks play an important role in the management and handling of money market investments for their parent institutions, as well as for the account of customers located outside the United States. In many cases the head office of the parent bank overseas advances funds to its New York branch or agency, which in turn invests these funds in the New York money market or loans these funds to customers located in the U.S. or elsewhere. In this connection at October 1973 the U.S. offices of foreign banks held $10.1 billion in funds due to parent banks or affiliated institutions outside the United States.

Over three-fourths of the $8 billion of short-term assets held in New York by foreign business firms and others was in the form of demand and time deposits. The remainder was held in money market assets. While detailed data is not published regarding the extent to which these dollar deposits of non-residents are placed with foreign banking offices in the U.S., scattered information that has been provided indicates that foreign banks obtain a major part of the total. It is difficult to ascertain what net contribution the presence of foreign banks makes to the international depository role of New York. However, it must be considerable with respect to funds placed in New York by foreign banks as well as foreign business firms.

3. CLEARING AND MONEY TRANSFER

The New York financial market plays an important role as a clearing centre and money transfer hub for the world economy. The presence of foreign banks in the U.S., especially their New York offices, adds to the ebb and flow of funds that pass through New York and expands the number of alternatives available to U.S. residents and non-residents in the management of their cash and liquidity positions.

4. ADVANTAGES OF FOREIGN BANKS IN NEW YORK

Foreign banks derive considerable advantages from a New York banking office. First, they enjoy the benefits of a low cost lending base. A comparison of dollar lending rates between the U.S. (the prime rate plus 15 per cent compensating balances) and London interbank offer rate (LIBO for 90 days) in the period 1966–73 indicates that the London rate was higher most of the time. Only in the periods 1967 (first half), 1970 (second half), and 1973 (second half) was the London rate lower than the U.S. prime lending rate. This indicates that in this period the New York lending base provided foreign banks with significant competitive advantages. Whether this same pattern will prevail in future cannot be ascertained at present.[15]

A second advantage for foreign banks is the increased flexibility of loan operations afforded with a New York (or U.S.) lending base. Foreign banks may lend from a home country base, a Eurodollar base, or a U.S. lending base. This flexibility includes cost and availability of funds, opportunity to benefit from time and space arbitrage, and the ability to broaden the scope of lending based upon the pattern of loan demand in each credit market region.

A third advantage for foreign banks represented in the U.S. is the ability to effect transactions for the parent bank or head office overseas. This includes money market transactions, direct loan activities, foreign exchange and clearing transactions, and foreign trade financing activities. A fourth advantage is the opportunity to bid for funds in a diverse multi-source money market.

Finally, foreign banking institutions find a dollar base of operations attractive due to the relatively unrestricted supply of funds available to them. This high elasticity of supply of dollar funds results from the pervasive importance of moneyed transactions in the U.S. economy, the relatively small portion of total funds absorbed by foreign banks, and the ability of foreign banks operating in the U.S. to bid more aggressively for dollar funds. This last point requires elaboration, which is provided in the following section.

D. ADVANTAGES OF FOREIGN BANKS OVER DOMESTIC

It has been argued that in the area of money market and credit market activities foreign banks enjoy several advantages over domestic banks. Two basic types of advantages must be considered in this context. First, it is held that foreign banks enjoy certain cost advantages over domestic banks in the U.S. The cost advantages relate to absence of FDIC insurance premiums, and lower costs from reserve requirements. Lower effective costs can permit foreign banks to bid more aggressively for money market and deposit sources of funds, as well as underbid on corporate and consumer loans. The second advantage is in the ability of foreign banks more effectively to arbitrage funds between the U.S. and offshore credit markets.

1. COST ADVANTAGES

The existence of significant cost advantages for foreign banks is important in several respects. First, it suggests 'unfair advantages' over domestic banking institutions, and the need to remedy an inequitable situation. Second, if they are substantial enough cost advantages permit foreign banks to overbid for lendable funds and/or underbid in making loans and investments. In both instances deposit, loan, and money market volume will gravitate to foreign banking institutions at the expense of domestic banks.

In the area of FDIC insurance premium assessments, it has been held that foreign banks do not incur such expenses and therefore are able to operate at an advantage compared with domestic banking institutions. We should note that agencies of foreign banks are not eligible to receive deposit funds and therefore cannot be considered as possessing any such advantage.[16] Under the Bank Holding Company Act state chartered subsidiaries of foreign banks are required to provide FDIC insurance and therefore enjoy no cost advantage. Branches of foreign banks operating in the United States are not eligible at present for FDIC insurance coverage, and can enjoy a cost advantage. The cost advantage must be related to the insurance premium assessment on total deposits paid to the FDIC by all insured banks. This cost advantage is equivalent to approximately three per cent of pretax net income of domestic insured banks and is not sufficient to provide any significant advantage for foreign banks that do not incur this cost.

A somewhat more important cost advantage probably can be found in the area of reserve requirements as they apply to foreign banks operating in the United States. In general states impose reserve requirements against deposit liabilities in banks that do not deviate widely from the percentage levels imposed by the Federal Reserve on member banks. In New York the same percentages apply to state nonmember banks subject to state reserve requirements and member banks (state chartered banks and national banks) subject to Federal Reserve requirements.

While the percentage reserve requirements are generally similar as between state and Federal Reserve requirements, there are important differences in the form in which required reserves may be held. The Federal Reserve considers vault cash or non-interest earning deposits at the Fed as eligible to satisfy reserve requirements. These cash assets produce no income and represent 'frozen assets' that contribute nothing to bank earnings.

State nonmember banks (including branches and most state chartered subsidiaries of foreign banks) can apply a wide list of assets to satisfy state reserve requirements. These assets include vault cash, clearing balances held with the Federal Reserve, and demand deposits in other banks. Some states permit reserves to be held in negotiable CDs, and cash items in process of collection. Twenty-three states (including California, Massachusetts, and Oregon) permit securities to be counted among eligible assets, and two states permit counting federal funds sold. The above points out clearly that the present structure of reserve requirements can create significant cost incentives for banks to remain nonmembers (Table 5-5). As a result a large Japanese owned state chartered bank withdrew from membership (Sumitomo Bank of California). At the time it was acquired by Lloyds Bank Ltd. of London (1973) the First Western Bank and Trust, Los Angeles was a nonmember bank.

The extent of advantage enjoyed by nonmember banks (including foreign owned banking institutions) varies from state to state. In New York where the greatest amount of deposits is concentrated in foreign banks the advantages are not significant. In addition to vault cash, New York treats funds 'due from banks' as eligible to satisfy state reserve requirements. By contrast, in California nonmember banks are permitted to hold up to four-fifths of reserves required on time and savings deposits in U.S. government securities. In periods of high or rising money market interest rates nonmember banks in California can earn a premium return on U.S. government securities held to satisfy reserve requirements on time and savings deposits.

2. ABILITY TO ARBITRAGE FUNDS

Foreign banks operating in the United States are in an excellent position to arbitrage funds between the principal money and credit markets. Moreover, the development of the Eurodollar market provides additional flexibility in this direction. This latter advantage is important in light of the difficulties frequently encountered by expatriate banks in generating local (host country) deposit sources of funds. Foreign banks can obtain Eurodollars, transfer these funds to U.S. branches or agencies, and build up a large base of loan activities, all without assuming any net foreign currency exposure position.

In the 1960s domestic banks in the U.S. found that foreign branches provided considerable flexibility, since they could obtain Eurodollar funds and advance them to their head offices for purposes of reserve adjustment. In October 1969 the Federal Reserve Board imposed a reserve requirement on balances due from domestic offices to their foreign branches and against foreign branch loans to U.S. residents. The purpose of this reserve requirement was to curb domestic credit creation supported by reserves obtained through the Eurodollar market.[17] An exception was made in the case of U.S. corporate borrowing from foreign branches of American banks, when these borrowings were loaned by the parent corporation to an overseas subsidiary. Such loans permitted the foreign investing corporation to comply with the rules of the Office of Foreign Direct Investment (OFDI), an agency of the U.S. Department of Commerce that administered the U.S. government regulations on direct investment dollar outflows.

In the period 1969–73 foreign banks enjoyed distinct international arbitrage of funds advantages over American banks.

Table 5-5

Reserve Requirements against Deposit Liabilities in Selected States

State	Deposits Subject to Reserve Requirement	Reserve Requirement Ratio Minimum	Maximum	Current	Vault Cash	Reserve Assets Eligible to Meet Requirements Due From Banks	U.S. Government Securities	Other Securities
California	Demand	n.a.	n.a.	8–18%[a]	x	x		
	Cash Items in Process of Collection							
	Time-Savings	n.a.	n.a.	8–18%[a] 5%	x Min. of 1/4	x Up to 3/4	Up to 4/5	
Hawaii	Demand			12%	Min. of 1/4	Up to 3/4		
	Time-Savings			5%				
Illinois	(NO STATUTORY REQUIREMENT)							
Massachusetts	Demand & Time Boston			20%	Min. of 15%	Up to 80%	Up to 80%	
	Elsewhere			15%				
New York	Demand Due From[b]			7–17%[a]				
	Cash Items in Process of Collection				x	x		
	Saving			3%	x	x		

State	Deposits Subject to Reserve Requirement	Reserve Requirement Ratio			Reserve Assets Eligible to Meet Requirements			
		Minimum	Maximum	Current	Vault Cash	Due From Banks	U.S. Government Securities	Other Securities
New York (*continued*)	Time & Time CD			8%	x	x		
Oregon	Demand			12%	x	x		
	Time-Savings			4%	x	x	x	
Washington	Demand	FR[c]	15%[a]	8–15%[a]	x	x		x
	Savings	FR	6%	3%	x	x		x
	Time	FR	6%	3–5%	x	x		

[a] Reserve requirements are applied in each tranche of deposits at successively higher percentages. Generally, deposits over $400 million carry the highest percentage requirement indicated.
[b] Demand deposits due from domestic banks.
[c] Percentage is same as Federal Reserve requirement.

Source: Federal Reserve Bank of Kansas City, *Monthly Review*, 'Reserve Requirements: Part I. Comparative Reserve Requirements at Member and Nonmember Banks', April 1974, pp. 15–20.

IMPACT ON U.S. BANKING AND FINANCE 69

American banks were restricted in the amount of foreign lending by Federal Reserve voluntary controls and the Interest Equalization Tax (flow 6 in Illustration 5-1). Moreover, American banks could not obtain Eurodollar funds (inflows) without their being subject to reserve requirements under Regulation M and Regulation D of the Federal Reserve Board (flows 1 and 3 in Illustration 5-1). By contrast, foreign banking offices in the U.S. not subject to Federal Reserve reserve requirements could borrow funds from their parent institutions for loan operations in the United States (flow 4 in Illustration 5-1). In 1973 this advantage was reduced when the Federal Reserve Board Chairman issued a letter to foreign banks requesting that they voluntarily adhere to the same reserve requirements applicable against foreign source funds of member banks.

In January 1974 improvement in the U.S. balance of payments position permitted removal of the foreign lending and investment restrictions imposed on U.S. banks and industrial corporations. The Interest Equalization Tax was removed and U.S. corporations were free to transfer funds to overseas subsidiaries without restriction. However in the following month the Federal Reserve Board announced that the exemption from reserve requirements of U.S. corporate borrowing from foreign branches of American banks was no longer applicable. In the past such loans to U.S. corporations had been granted exemption from the Regulation M reserve requirements based on the need to comply with OFDI rules limiting transfers of funds to foreign subsidiaries of U.S. corporations that were harmful to the U.S. balance of payments (flows 1a and 5 in Illustration 5-1). Beginning in February 1974 only loans made directly by foreign branches of American banks to overseas subsidiaries of U.S. companies (flow 2 in Illustration 5-1), and loans made by U.S. bank head offices to overseas subsidiaries (flow 6 in Illustration 5-1) were exempt from reserve requirements.

For reasons of international tax strategy, or due to other reasons, a U.S. multinational corporation may prefer to carry out the borrowing itself rather than through a foreign subsidiary. For this reason more corporate borrowers have been turning to the head offices of foreign banks for Eurodollar loan funds. Head offices of foreign banks are not subject to reserve requirements of the Federal Reserve (higher costs), and therefore may be able to charge lower interest rates. The loan to the U.S. company may be booked in the foreign banks head office, even though the U.S. branch or agency of the foreign institution negotiated the loan. As previously noted, U.S. branches or agencies of foreign banks may not be subject to Federal Reserve jurisdiction where reserve requirements are concerned, but will follow Fed reserve requirements since there is 'moral suasion'.

Under conditions of monetary ease in the United States the arbitrage advantages of foreign banks would be minimal. Given the vast petrodollar flow expected to move into the Eurodollar

Illustration 5-1

Arbitrage Opportunities for Foreign and U.S. Banks

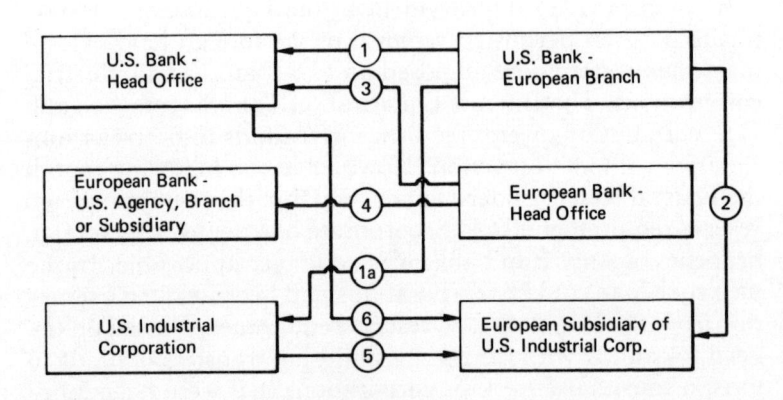

Legend:
1. U.S. member bank must maintain reserve requirement against balance due to foreign branches, and foreign branch loans to U.S. residents under Regulation M. In 1973–74 this requirement was set at 8 per cent of such balances.
2. No reserve requirements apply to loans made by overseas branches of U.S. banks to overseas affiliates of U.S. companies.
3. U.S. member bank must maintain reserve against balance due to foreign banks under Regulation D. In 1973–74 this requirement was set at 8 per cent of such balances.
4. The Federal Reserve Board has asked foreign banks located in the U.S. to voluntarily conform to reserve requirements relative to borrowings from parent or affiliated institutions overseas. The amount requested in 1973–74 was 8 per cent of such balances.

5. American parent corporate loan to overseas subsidiary. No reserve requirement applies.
6. U.S. bank lending restricted by Federal Reserve administered voluntary controls and by IET. In effect until January 1974.

market, lower interest rates may persist in that financial market sector for a considerable period of time. Considering the reserve requirement advantages discussed above, this interest rate shift could seriously undermine the competitive position of American banks in servicing U.S. corporate cash requirements.

In the highly competitive Eurodollar market loans retail to corporate borrowers at a narrow margin above the wholesale rate that applies to interbank dealing. The foreign branch of an American bank that borrows Eurodollars relends them in the U.S. with an added cost equivalent to the 8 per cent reserve requirement imposed on U.S. head office borrowings from overseas branches. At Eurodollar rates prevailing in October 1974 (10.50 per cent) the cost of the 8 per cent reserve requirement works out to approximately 91 basis points of additional interest cost, bringing the total cost of funds to 11.41 per cent. Considering the extremely narrow profit margin in the Eurodollar market, the reserve requirement represents a formidable barrier against loans by London branches of American banks to U.S. corporations. If we consider the possibility of the head office of the U.S. bank offering customers domestic funds, the prime rate and compensating balance measures the cost of funds to the borrower. In October 1974 the prime rate in the U.S. was 11.25 per cent. If we assume compensating balances of 15 per cent the effective cost of funds to the U.S. customer is 13.25 per cent, considerably above that of Eurodollar funds provided via foreign branches of American banks. A foreign bank could offer the U.S. borrower a Eurodollar loan at the straight London Eurodollar offer rate of 10.50 per cent.

6 Multinational Portfolio Management

> My ventures are not in one bottom trusted
> Nor to one place.
>
> *The Merchant of Venice*

A. GROWING SCOPE OF INVESTMENT OPERATIONS IN UNITED STATES

In the period 1960–74 the scope of international investment operations has expanded at a quickening pace. This expansion has been achieved despite the appearance of new and formidable obstacles such as U.S. controls on capital flows, a world monetary crisis, and global inflation. At the forefront of this expanded international investment activity have been the multinational banks of American, European and Japanese nationality. The widened scope of international investment, in part an outgrowth of the internationalisation of business and banking, has generated a need for better understanding of the effects and influences from foreign investment. In the United States the Congress passed into law the Foreign Investment Study Act of 1974. This Act directs the Secretary of Commerce and Secretary of the Treasury to 'conduct a comprehensive, overall study of foreign direct and portfolio investment in the United States'.

Multinational portfolio management involves servicing the global investment needs of the big banks, industrial corporations, and private investors who have found it profitable to hold assets that are dispersed across a large number of nations. This chapter examines the field of multinational portfolio management in connection with the role played by foreign banks operating in the United States.

Table 6-1
Calculation of Expected Return and Dispersion on Return from an Investment in U.S. by a Foreign Bank

1 Alternative States of the World	2 Probability Factor p	3 Return Anticipated on Investment X	4 Calculation of Expected Return pX	5a [X − E(X)]	5b Calculation of Dispersion [X − E(X)]²	5c p[X − E(X)]²
Pessimistic	.3	−.040	−.140	−.140	.0196	.00588
Moderate	.5	.200	.100	.100	.0100	.00500
Optimistic	.2	.060	.012	.040	.0016	.00032
			E(X) = .100			Var(X) = .01120
E(X) = 10% ϭ = 10.5%						ϭ = .105

1. ANALYTIC MODEL OF RISK-RETURN RELATION IN FOREIGN INVESTMENT

A major problem confronting business and banking operations is making decisions under conditions of risk. International banking and business activities are exposed to a wider range of risks than domestic activities. The return versus risk relationships generally are measured in terms of expected returns and standard deviation of returns. In this section the concepts of expected return and variation in return are explained by means of numerical relationships described within the context of investment selection under conditions of risk.

A foreign bank or business firm contemplating an investment in a U.S. operation can evaluate the proposal in terms of the most probable return. This requires analysis of the probabilities of alternative possible returns summarised by an average value and the dispersion around this average. Computations for the expected return from a foreign bank's investment in the U.S. and its dispersion are found in Table 6-1. In Columns 1 and 2 alternative future states of the world are described along with their probability factors. In Column 3 we see the alternative returns possible under different possible states of the world. Under optimistic conditions, which have a probability of 0.20, the foreign bank may expect a return of 6 per cent.

In Column 4 the probabilities of the alternative state of the world are multiplied by the possible outcomes (returns). By summing Column 4 we obtain an expected return of 10 per cent for the U.S. investment. The expected return is the relevant criterion. However, we must also consider a measure of dispersion or risk. One possible measure is the range of possible returns, which in this case is (0.200— —0.040) or 0.240. The range of returns is 24 per cent. Two other measures of dispersion or risk are calculated in Table 6-1. These are the variance and standard deviation, for which calculations are shown in Columns 5a, 5b, and 5c. The variance is the weighted sum of the squared deviations. The square root of the variance is the standard deviation. An important use of the standard deviation hinges on its statistical property of judging the likelihood of future events. In general the results of future events are likely to fall between values of plus and minus two standard deviations from the expected value. Therefore, the 10.5 per cent standard deviation of the foreign bank's investment return in the U.S. could allow for a more than doubling of the expected return or significant losses. As measured by the standard deviation the foreign bank's investment in the U.S. carried a high degree of risk (10.5 per cent).

The foregoing is not meant to signify that foreign investments necessarily involve a greater degree of risk than domestic investments. This may or may not be the case, depending upon the specific investments.

In evaluating or appraising the risk associated with foreign investments we must distinguish between the degree of risk inherent in a specific investment, and the effect this foreign investment has on the overall risk position of the foreign investor. Assume that a European bank enjoys the risk-return relation on its domestic investment indicated in Table 6-2, where it can earn 10 per cent at a risk of 5 per cent (standard deviation). A contemplated foreign investment (say in the U.S.) will yield a higher (12 per cent) return, but with a commensurately higher risk (10 per cent standard deviation). If we consider the domestic and foreign investments taken together as constituting an investment portfolio, the overall risk-return relationships can be calculated on the global portfolio. As we can see, the foreign investment (establishment of a U.S. branch or subsidiary) increases the average return, and lowers the risk on the global portfolio below even that associated with the parent bank's domestic operations in its home country. The reduction of risk on the global portfolio is achieved through efficient diversification of that portfolio.

Table 6-2

Risk–Return Relationships on Domestic, Foreign, and Global Investment Portfolio

	Return	Risk
Domestic Investment	10%	5%
Foreign Investment	12%	10%
Global Portfolio	11%	4%

When we analyse the many activities of a business firm from the standpoint of portfolio management, the foreign activities of a firm may be regarded as aiming at diversification. Foreign banks and business firms may broaden their portfolios so as to achieve efficient diversification. Efficient diversification may be defined as the minimisation of risk to achieve a given expected return. Alternately, efficient diversification can be achieved by holding the level of risk fixed and obtaining the highest expected return available from various portfolio combinations. In an economy with well developed financial markets, business and bank investors may better focus on maximising returns within a prescribed field of activity, letting individual investors diversify through the financial markets. This is due to the low level of transactions costs (brokerage commissions and transfer taxes) to the individual investor. However, where financial markets are not well developed business firms and banks may pursue efficient diversification by means of extending the scope of their investments, and international operations may prove the best avenue of approach. Moreover, business firms and banks may achieve efficient portfolio diversification and achieve synergy as well. To achieve synergy complementary benefits or economies of scale must be present.[1]

To achieve the benefits of portfolio diversification it is necessary that the activities relating to different investments be not perfectly positively correlated. The data incorporated in Table 6-2 illustrate the effects from efficient portfolio diversification. The expected return on the global portfolio is the weighted average of the returns on the investments in the portfolio. However, the standard deviation or risk of the portfolio is much reduced below the degree of risk applicable to each of the component investments. This risk reduction takes place because of the low or negative correlation between the returns available from the two investments.[2]

The preceding analysis in our analytic model suggests that foreign banks and business firms can benefit from investments in the United States (and elsewhere). These benefits are more clearly seen after examining the risk-return analysis and principles of efficient portfolio diversification outlined above.

2. DATA ON FOREIGN DIRECT INVESTMENT

The discussion which follows occupies a central place in the understanding of why and how many foreign banks have been attracted to the United States. Essentially, it is keyed to an implicit understanding that banks, as well as trade, follow the flag. In this sense the flag is borne by the industrial corporation and trading affiliates of home country business firms, whose patronage and clientele foreign banks are seeking to retain.

The theoretical explanation for foreign direct investment flows into the United States includes monopolistic imperfections in industry structure, the need for the firm to maintain satisfactory growth, and capital market imperfections that provide opportunities for better returns on control as compared with portfolio investments.[3] According to data published by the U.S. Department of Commerce, the acceleration in direct investment flows coming into the United States (1967–72) was assisted by growth of the Eurodollar market and the possibility of financing U.S. investments from this liquid pool of funds, the 1967 Securities and Exchange Commission action which modified its rules regarding financial reporting of foreign owned U.S. firms (allowing use of accounting practices more in line with those used by foreign parent companies), and the merger movement among European firms.[4]

The dollar devaluations of 1971 and 1973 coupled with the downward stock market trend in the period 1972–74 have made U.S. investments more attractive to foreign business firms. This is evidenced by a survey completed by The Conference Board in 1974, which indicated that in the first quarter of 1974 foreign firms had announced plans to invest over $340 million in U.S. manufacturing facilities. Also, in the one year period March 1973 to March 1974 foreign firms revealed intentions to spend over $3.5 billion on U.S. manufacturing facilities.

The leading direct investor countries in the U.S. have been the United Kingdom, Canada, the Netherlands, Switzerland, Germany, Belgium-Luxembourg, France, and Sweden. Japan is conspicuous by its absence from the top ranked countries in 1971 (Table 6-3). Japan's direct investments in the U.S. remained close to $100 million in the period 1962–67. In the years 1968–70 there was a significant increase, which was more than reversed in 1971 as Japanese trading firms in the U.S. prepaid parent companies for imports.

With the exception of Japan, countries that have taken the lead in direct investment activity in the United States, also tend to lead in home country bank representation in the U.S. This close correlation between status as a direct investor and importance of home country banking representation in the United States is no accident.

Table 6-3

Foreign Direct Investments in the United States

	Millions of dollars		
	1962	1967	1971
Value of Direct Investment at Yearend:			
Total	7,612	9,923	13,704
United Kingdom	2,474	3,156	4,435
Canada	2,064	2,575	3,339
Netherlands	1,082	1,508	2,225
Switzerland	836	1,096	1,537
Germany	152	318	767
Belgium–Luxembourg	158	228	341
France	183	265	315
Sweden	179	239	229
By Industry:			
Petroleum	1,419	1,885	3,113
Manufacturing	2,885	4,181	6,748
Trade	750	848	568
Insurance & Finance	1,943	2,193	2,352

Source: U.S. Department of Commerce, *Survey of Current Business*, February 1973.

It is not surprising to find that manufacturing accounts for close to fifty per cent of foreign direct investment in the United States. Petroleum investment ranks second, having passed the insurance and finance category in 1969. Many states limit or prohibit foreign ownership of banks, and this contributed to the decline in share of total investment represented by insurance and finance.[5]

In 1971 the earnings of direct investors in the United States was estimated at $1,110 million, of which $623 million took the form of interest and dividend payments to parent companies and branch earnings. It is clear from these figures, as well as from those pertaining to value of direct investments, that a considerable foreign exchange flow is generated in the form of remittance to parent companies, and that a substantial base of bank servicing business is available to home country banking institutions.

3. BANK SERVICING

A major consideration for foreign banks entering the United States has been the desire to service home country business firms. In 1971 and 1972 the total value of direct foreign investments in the U.S. was $13.7 billion and $14.3 billion, indicating that there now exists a wide base of corporate loan, deposit, specialty finance, underwriting, money transfer, and foreign trade financing business for home country banks operating from a U.S. base. Servicing the broader base of foreign portfolio and direct investment in the U.S., foreign banks have made use of securities affiliates that engage in underwriting, securities trading, and portfolio management activities. As a result, some of the U.S. activities of foreign banks follow the British merchant bank model.

Merchant banking refers to the diversified financial activities of approximately two dozen, old-line British banks. In the past these merchant banks have focused on three lines of business, including banking (deposit, loans, acceptances and export credit), company services (mergers, specialty finance and underwriting), and portfolio management (stock exchange investments for individual investors and institutions). Merchant banks are important in raising venture capital, development finance, leasing, factoring, and bullion dealing. American banks are permitted to engage in many aspects of merchant banking, with the exception of securities underwriting and broker-dealer operations on the stock exchange.

A dozen of the leading British merchant banks now have direct representation in New York, and one of the largest New York merchant bank affiliates, Schroder, Naess & Thomas, has branch offices in principal cities such as Washington, D.C., Atlanta and Baltimore. In addition, the Schroder Group has representative offices in Brazil, Argentina, Germany, and

Canada; and minority interests in affiliates in Australia, Beirut, Hong Kong, Spain and Ireland.

The Schroder, Naess and Thomas affiliate in New York is the pivot affiliate in the United States. It is a bank holding company subject to the supervision of the Board of Governors of the Federal Reserve System. In turn, Schroder, Naess & Thomas owns the J. Henry Schroder Banking Corp which conducts a foreign banking and investment advisory business. This bank in turn owns the Schroder Trust Company which is a member of the Federal Reserve System.

An important aspect of the Schroder Group activities in the United States involves investment management. In 1971 it was reported that Schroder, Naess & Thomas was managing $800 million in portfolio assets. This includes management of three investment companies of which one (American Investment Trust, N.V.) is a closed end trust. In addition, Schroder Trust Company manages a closed end investment company (International Holdings Corporation). The Federal Reserve has ruled that management of domestic investment companies is permissible for BHCs, and Regulation Y issued by the Board of Governors permits banks to serve as investment advisors to registered investment companies.

B. FOREIGN BANKING INSTITUTIONS IN THE U.S. SECURITIES MARKETS

1. NEEDS OF FOREIGN BANKS

It is necessary to consider the differences between banking abroad and banking in the United States before we can fully appreciate the importance of investment banking and securities operations of foreign banks in the United States. Many big banks in Europe derive a considerable share of their business from securities trading, underwriting, and portfolio management activities.

For the American reader this discussion could be made more emphatic if we considered a combination of Chase Manhattan Bank and Merrill, Lynch, Pierce, Fenner and Smith. A combination of this type would bring together a leading commercial bank and the largest securities brokerage firm in the United States. At present a combination of this type in the U.S. lies far beyond the borders of reality, and for this reason indicates the divergent views of U.S. and European policy-makers concerning the appropriate structuring and competitive relationships that should prevail in the financial markets.

Foreign banks that participate actively in the U.S. securities markets do so because of the need to maintain a well-rounded global business. This requires that these banks be permitted to carry out all of the types of activities they engage in at home. Failure to service long-standing customers by operating directly in the U.S. markets might lose customer loyalty and the ability to continue servicing these clients in other important phases of banking.

The operating areas which foreign banks have found it necessary to service by means of U.S. securities affiliates include the following: (1) customer transactions in U.S. securities, (2) listing and trading foreign securities on the New York Stock Exchange, and (3) participating in underwriting of issues.

The volume of foreign purchases and sales of U.S. equity securities has grown impressively. In the two year period 1972–73 the net increase of foreign holdings of U.S. equities via purchases and sales averaged $2.5 billion, more than the gross purchases or sales of foreign investors a decade earlier (1963).[6] The New York Stock Exchange (NYSE) has reported that in the period 1956–70 the number of foreign shareowners of listed shares increased by 1,150 per cent. These impressive figures indicate a substantial base of foreign investor transactions which home country and other banks specialised in securities operations can benefit from. Taking the volume of foreign purchase orders reflected in gross purchases in 1973, the brokerage commissions generated on the NYSE would have been in excess of $100 million.[7]

A second need of foreign banks is to provide for the listing and trading in foreign securities. At yearend 1973 the value of foreign securities listed on the NYSE was $20.1 billion of which $17.7 billion represented stocks. Over 35 per cent of these securities represent those of European companies and government borrowers. Among the listed foreign stocks are included such actively traded issues as British Petroleum, Distillers Corp.-Seagrams, International Nickel, KLM, Roan Selection Trust, Schlumberger, Sony and Unilever. In 1973 gross transactions in foreign stocks reached $1.7 billion of foreign purchases and $1.5 billion of foreign sales, yielding net sales to foreigners of $175 million.

Finally, the U.S. underwriting activities of foreign securities firms provides their parent banks with the ability to service corporate and other customers in a highly efficient capital market. This is especially important considering the scrapping of the Interest Equalisation Tax by the U.S. government early in 1974, and in light of the growing financing requirements of foreign corporations establishing production facilities in the United States.

2. OPPORTUNITIES IN U.S. FINANCIAL MARKETS

Foreign banks have found opportunities that might appear to be far greater than is warranted by the size of the U.S. financial system. There are several reasons for this. First, artificial restrictions in the form of legislation and government regulation hamper the ready entry of new competitors, thus providing the lure of a potentially large volume of new business to firms able to successfully enter these lines of activity. Second, restrictions on access to stock market trading by the New York Stock Exchange and member firm organisations have prevented the development of competition by foreign securities firms and affiliates of foreign banks. The Lorie Report on the American capital markets notes that some of the regional exchanges accept foreign members. It further suggests that 'Foreign firms should have direct access to the new central market system'.[8] The Report notes two exceptions to this recommendation, in cases of negotiating for reciprocal privileges for American securities firms, and in cases where foreign banks operate securities affiliates.

Studies prepared for the NYSE have consistently recommended that U.S. brokerage affiliates of foreign companies and foreign banks be prohibited from direct access to U.S. stock exchanges through membership, or indirect access through the professional commission discount on non-member firm transactions for their public transactions.[9] The question of foreign membership has been under close scrutiny since 1973, and it has been reported that there are good prospects for some revision in membership policy. Since many countries (Switzerland and Germany) lodge their securities business in banks that conduct a mixed business, attempts to gain reciprocity from these countries for U.S. securities firms would have to include allowing the securities affiliates of banks from these countries membership on the U.S. stock exchanges.

The removal of fixed commissions on the NYSE could dampen the enthusiasm of foreign firms seeking a seat on the NYSE so as to recapture commissions going to member firms. The Securities and Exchange Commission has taken the position that the securities markets in the United States will be best served if broad broker–dealer participation is encouraged. The Lorie Report prepared for the U.S. Treasury Department has advocated that the U.S. take the initiative in providing a freer climate for international operations of securities firms.

Practical difficulties enter into the question of foreign firm representation on the stock markets in areas such as effective regulation and equal competition. It is difficult to integrate U.S. capital market methods and structures with the different kinds of market operations that predominate overseas. The securities markets and stock exchanges in Europe are organised in very different ways. For example, in most European markets the banks do almost all of the trading in equity securities. In the United States this kind of brokerage activity is prohibited by the Glass-Steagall Act. If membership of foreign firms is permitted on the U.S. stock exchanges to what extent would American banks be placed at a competitive disadvantage? Many of the close to thirty foreign brokerage firms operating in New York are owned by foreign banks. If they should become eligible for stock exchange membership, U.S. banks would seek to enjoy that same advantage. It is remotely possible that American banks could achieve stock exchange membership in the U.S. via their foreign affiliates. U.S. banks currently participate in the brokerage business overseas by means of affiliate firms. The same U.S. banks could save considerable stock brokerage commissions paid to U.S. securities firms by gaining stock exchange membership for these foreign affiliates.[10]

In many countries foreign firms are prohibited from doing business in the domestic stock market. Even where formal restrictions do not exist (Switzerland) U.S. securities firms are discouraged from joining the stock exchanges. More important, U.S. brokerage firms may be permitted to operate in a given country only if they agree not to solicit business of individual investors. The U.S. could undertake a reciprocal liberalisation of membership and access to trading facilities with other countries. However, numerous problems would remain unanswered. First, would the U.S. be giving up more than it could possibly gain from a reciprocal open door policy? The U.S. securities market is vastly greater than any of its overseas counterparts. Second, would a reciprocal open door policy enlarge the advantages foreign banks enjoy over American banks in being able to participate in the U.S. securities business while American banks are prohibited from doing so?

The separation of commercial banking from investment banking in the United States, which is codified in the Glass-Steagall provision of the Banking Act of 1933, provides considerable opportunities for foreign banks and bank affiliated brokerage firms. American banks are prohibited from underwriting new securities issues (except for government securities) and from engaging in securities brokerage and trading. In effect, there is a partial separation of the securities markets in the United States whereby domestic commercial banks are enjoined from supporting the markets for corporate securities by direct purchases, by providing brokerage facilities, or by underwriting corporate securities. This contrasts sharply with the situation in other advanced countries where large banks enjoy stock exchange membership, dominate the new issues business, and invest in corporate equities and long-term debt securities.

The partial separation of securities markets in the United States tends to weaken the market sectors that commercial banks are prohibited from entering. Weakness in the equity market has been a point of special concern in recent years, especially since the strong bull market of 1968 and the dismal performance of the stock market in the period 1969–74. Since 1969 there has been a steady erosion of the dealer organisation,[11] an inability to improve or even maintain stock exchange member firm capital accounts relative to total assets, extreme fluctuations in stock exchange member firm profitability, and a decline in the price of membership (seat) on the NYSE.[12]

The entry of foreign bank securities affiliates into the stock market offsets the weakening influence that follows from Glass-Steagall prohibitions against domestic bank participation in the securities business. Unfortunately, this alone is not sufficient reason to remove such prohibitions. Removal of the Glass-Steagall prohibition against U.S. bank participation in the securities business is a complicated issue, and would have to be placed in juxtaposition with conflicting goals including avoidance of monopolistic influence in the financial markets and safety of bank deposit funds. What is important in our discussion is that the existence of Glass-Steagall restrictions on domestic bank activities in the securities markets has left a partial vacuum that foreign banks have sought to enter. It is possible that the U.S. Congress may see fit to leave the Glass-Steagall restriction on the books so as to preserve the integrity of deposit funds and to avoid development of a 'money trust'. However, the American lawmakers may further decide to inject new competition and venture capital into the corporate securities markets by sanctioning the admission of foreign securities firms to full stock exchange membership. For purposes of achieving equal treatment, the foreign based securities affiliates of U.S. commercial banks may also be permitted to gain a small foothold in the U.S. capital market by means of more liberal access to stock exchange trading activity.

3. FOREIGN BANK PARTICIPATION AND SERVICING OF MULTINATIONAL PORTFOLIO MANAGEMENT

Concern over the growing penetration of the U.S. financial markets by foreign banks raises serious questions concerning the relative advantages of this new competition. In the area of portfolio management is it possible to arrive at an appraisal of the merits and costs of this penetration? Foreign bank penetration into portfolio management activities in the United States can be defended on several grounds.

It can be argued that the only effective institutional machinery available to prudently channel foreign funds into U.S. portfolio investments consists of the large European banks and British merchant banks. No ready alternative exists that possesses the expertise and ability to understand the sophisticated and complex American securities markets, unless we consider

American portfolio managers. We should remember that in Western Europe there is no institutional framework analogous to the specialised securities houses that operate on Wall Street. Only Japan possesses this type of institutional mechanism, and this is largely an outgrowth of the postwar military occupation and influence of American military advisers who wished to transplant the type of financial mechanism they were familiar with.

Foreign banks, especially the big banks in Germany, Switzerland, Belgium and the Netherlands are able to compete effectively with the largest American banks in the area of multinational portfolio management. This includes marketing, distributing and managing special mutual funds; providing for the safekeeping, handling and transfer of securities; executing trades of listed securities; and providing investment advisory services to customers. The export of liquid investment capital by American residents, partly related to currency uncertainties and inflation in the United States, has provided the European banks with an opportunity to take on new American customers, much to the chagrin of U.S. mutual fund managers, commercial bank trust departments, and investment advisors.

We can further defend foreign bank participation in portfolio management activities in the United States on the grounds that it results in net inflows of investment funds that strengthen the U.S. balance of payments. In this connection, removal of the Interest Equalization Tax early in 1974 should provide opportunities for substantial two-way flows of investment capital. This will follow from the ability of foreign borrowers to sell dollar bond issues in the U.S. capital market, simultaneously attracting foreign investment funds to purchase a substantial portion of such issues.

The prospects of an expanding role for foreign banks and their securities affiliates in New York raises several questions regarding the function to be played by this centre in international portfolio management.

1. Should foreign banks be given relative freedom to operate securities and underwriting affiliates in New York on the basis that this will tend to reinforce New York's position as an international portfolio centre?

2. To what extent is it possible to relax existing restrictions on American bank securities business activities so as to equalise their competitive position relative to foreign banks operating in this field in the U.S.?
3. Should American banks be permitted to organise or own foreign securities affiliates that operate in the U.S.? This would place American banks on a competitive par with foreign banks, and also permit a much needed injection of equity capital in the securities industry in the U.S.
4. What effect will an expanding base of foreign banks in New York's securities industry have on the brokerage commission structure, practices followed in charging for investment research services, regulation of fees, charges levied by banks in cases of bank administered trust funds, and the sharing of regulatory jurisdiction by the Securities and Exchange Commission?
5. Will an expanded role of foreign banks in securities and underwriting operations in New York facilitate that centre's functioning as a major conduit for recycling the massive flows of petro-dollars expected to be generated over the next decade?

C. PETRO-DOLLAR RECYCLING

The scope of multinational portfolio management has and will continue to be affected by the large accumulation of investible reserves in the hands of petroleum exporting countries. As of mid-1975 projections were that the oil exporting countries could anticipate annual payments surpluses of $50–60 billion in 1975–76, but that these surpluses could disappear and become deficits by 1979. It has been further estimated that the OPEC nations could accumulate monetary reserves of approximately $200–250 billion by 1979. The lion's share would be owned by five countries (Saudi Arabia, Libya, Kuwait, Qatar, and AbuDhabi). If the rate of return on these investments was to average 10 per cent per annum the OPEC earnings might be in the neighbourhood of $20–25 billion annually by 1979.

How will the OPEC countries invest these reserves, and will the management of these funds result in stabilising or destabilising the international monetary and banking framework?

Will the United States financial markets attract a large share of these investible funds, and what role might foreign banks play in this direction?

Developments at yearend 1974 suggest that New York and the U.S. financial markets will play an important role in petrodollar recycling. Bank of England estimates indicate that during 1974 the OPEC countries accumulated investments and liquid reserves of $56 billion (Table 6-4). Some $21 billion of this was accumulated in U.K. institutions, including the foreign currency deposit market (Eurodollars) in London. Approximately $11 billion was invested in the U.S. financial markets. The remainder was invested in the Eurocurrency market outside of London, loaned through special bilateral facilities, and channelled through international organisations.

Two problems emerge when we consider the mechanics of recycling petro-dollars channelled into the United States. The large U.S. commercial banks have found their capital adequacy under strain, and have experienced difficulty in relending oil funds to borrowers in countries facing deepening balance of payments deficits (induced in part by enlarged oil import bills). In effect, large commercial banks in the United States are not in a position to serve as the sole or major recycling device. U.S. government securities have functioned as an alternative investment in the U.S. for petro-dollars. In short, these funds have been invested in the U.S. mainly in liquid assets, that can be sold readily. This complicates the management of monetary policy, but also shifts the burden onto the U.S. government to relend these funds abroad. To what extent can the U.S. government assume the credit risk involved in rechannelling oil revenues to borrowers in other countries? This difficulty could be surmounted if holders of U.S. government securities could be induced to shift their asset holdings to other U.S. capital market assets and if some investors holding U.S. capital market assets could be induced to acquire foreign loan assets.

The role of foreign banks in this recycling process could be critical. A European, Canadian, or Japanese bank could be in a better position than a U.S. bank to make foreign (non-U.S.) loans. This would especially be the case if the loan was extended to a borrower in the foreign banks home country. Numerous questions persist. (1) Would New York become more attractive as a petro-dollar lending base for foreign banks? (2) In what manner would foreign banks operating in

Table 6-4
Estimated Deployment of Oil Producer Funds 1974

	Billions of U.S. Dollars
United Kingdom	
1. Sterling investments including bank deposits and government securities	6.0
2. Foreign currency deposits	13.8
3. Other foreign currency borrowing	1.2
4. Subtotal	21.0
United States	
5. Government and agency securities	6.0
6. Bank deposits	4.0
7. Other[a]	1.0
8. Subtotal	11.0
Other Countries	
9. Foreign currency deposits	9.0
10. Special bilateral facilities and other investments[b]	11.6
11. Subtotal	20.6
12. International organizations	3.6
13. TOTAL	56.2

[a] Includes holdings of equities and property.
[b] Includes loans to less developed countries.
Source: Bank of England.

the United States be able to acquire petro-dollar funds?[13] (3) How might the U.S. regulatory authorities view the growing role of foreign banks in rechannelling petro-dollars?

At present many observers view the United States financial markets as likely to carry a substantial part of the burden of recycling investible oil revenues. Removal of the IET in 1974, and U.S. government plans to lighten the tax burden on foreign investors whose funds 'pass through' the United States, could make New York an important centre for the redistribution of petro-dollars. Therefore, a New York operating base becomes a vital part of a foreign bank's global operation. A foreign bank in the U.S. could extend foreign loans. The foreign bank assumes the credit and currency risks. However, U.S. bank regulatory authorities might be unwilling to permit American depositors to suffer excessive indirect exposure from recycling activities. The volume of petro-dollar recycling may increase total foreign lending exposure beyond limits considered prudent by American bank regulatory authorities. This is especially important in the aftermath of the Franklin National Bank debacle, the Bankhaus I.D. Herstatt failure, and the failure of several small private banks in West Germany. It is possible that as foreign banks involve themselves extensively in petro-dollar recycling through their U.S. branches and subsidiaries U.S. regulatory authorities would reappraise their attitude toward foreign banks and impose additional safeguards to protect American depositors in these institutions. However, an increase in the underwriting activities of securities affiliates of foreign banks might not be considered as clear and present a danger to the integrity of the U.S. financial mechanism.

If the U.S. financial markets are to function as an international recycling channel for petro-dollars regulatory authorities will have to re-examine the institutional arrangements and patterns of doing business in the new issues markets. Numerous obstacles presently stand in the way of New York functioning as a new issues market. These include the relatively limited experience of American investors in foreign issues, regulatory limits on the amount of foreign securities issues that can be held by financial institutions, and an underwriting and dealer organisation that has been decimated (as to numbers and invested capital) in the period 1969–74.

D. U.S. POLICY AND FOREIGN INVESTMENT FLOWS

The economic policy of the U.S. government toward private foreign investment flows has gone through several states of transition. In the decade prior to 1960 the Truman and Eisenhower administrations were favourably disposed toward an increase in the flow of U.S. private investment to the rest of the world. The dollar was in scarce supply around the world, and reconstruction and development needs in Europe and the less developed countries were critical. Beginning around 1961 in the Kennedy administration serious attention focused on the balance of payments costs of foreign investment outflows. In 1962 Congress passed a Revenue Act which tightened up on the taxation of foreign investment income of U.S. companies. In 1964 the Interest Equalization Tax was enacted, and in 1965 voluntary controls were imposed on direct investment of U.S. companies and on U.S. bank lending abroad. The period 1960–73 was one in which foreign investment was viewed as costly in terms of the balance of payments effects.

It is possible that beginning in 1974 U.S. policy may be entering a new phase in the treatment of foreign investment flows. In this new phase Washington policy-makers may view the U.S. financial markets as playing an intermediary role, in which foreign lenders and foreign investors could make use of American financial institutions and markets to fulfill an important financial intermediation function. Several developments since 1973 reflect this new outlook:

1. In 1973 oil exporting nations raised selling prices of petroleum exports, accelerating the growth of their monetary reserves.
2. In January 1974 the U.S. government removed all capital controls that had been in effect, including the IET and controls on bank lending to non-residents.
3. During 1974 the U.S. Congress has been considering elimination of the withholding tax on interest and dividends paid to foreigners. At present the law requires that 30 per cent of such investment income be withheld at the source on payments abroad. It is believed that banks and brokers in New York would derive substantial benefits from such a development, since such taxes reduce the appeal to foreigners to hold investments in the United States.

Various government policy measures could be used to assist American and foreign banks in attracting foreign investment into the United States. Government policy makers will have to evaluate the 'costs' inherent in giving domestic or foreign banks relatively greater advantages in attracting foreign investment funds into the United States, in comparison with the greater or lesser 'productivity' or returns, as measured by the number of dollars of additional foreign investment inflow generated by these measures.

Foreign banks can make important contributions to the U.S. economy, and one form this contribution may take is in their ability to attract an inflow of foreign investment capital. In an environment of global inflation the U.S. capital markets may be extremely short of capital funds for many years to come. In future foreign banks may make an important contribution to the viability and stability of the U.S. capital markets by widening the scope of multinational portfolio management as well as increasing the net inflow of foreign investment capital.

III
POLICY ISSUES

7 Regulatory Issues and Alternatives

> Laws are like cobwebs, which may catch small flies,
> but let wasps and hornets break through.
>
> Jonathan Swift

The current regulatory treatment of foreign banks in the United States is a patchwork of overlapping jurisdiction in limited areas, juxtaposed against a wide gap at the federal level. Regulation of foreign banking in the United States has developed at an uneven pace, largely as a reaction to a problem situation. The general philosophy in the United States is that banking is sacrosanct, and must be protected (even against itself). Where Britain and the European Continent use suasion, America has substituted statute. In the sections which follow we describe the existing system of regulation, consider the problems perceived in the present regulatory treatment, analyse recent proposals to modify the regulation of foreign banks, and consider possible directions of approach.

A. PRESENT REGULATORY SYSTEM

At present foreign banks are subject to state and federal laws as they apply to domestic banking corporations. For the most part the United States has not applied special legislative or supervisory authority over foreign banks operating within its borders. Only a small number of states specifically authorise the establishment of foreign bank offices. New York and California license branches and agencies of foreign banks. Illinois and Massachusetts also permit foreign bank branches. Foreign banks have chartered state affiliates in New York, California, and Illinois.

The federal government has remained silent on the matter of foreign bank operations. Only in a few areas does existing federal law designed to deal with domestic banks become applicable to foreign banking institutions. The 1970 Bank Holding Company Act placed a number of foreign banks in BHC status, and simultaneously provided foreign banks with a workable statutory and administrative framework for expanding their operations in the U.S.[1]

1. NEW YORK STATE

New York has shouldered a major part of the responsibility for chartering, licensing and supervising foreign banks doing business in the United States. Consequently, the laws, administrative procedures, and experience gained in this direction constitute the most significant body of regulatory control and knowledge presently available in the United States.

While New York embraces a major part of the foreign bank resources located in the United States, its banking laws have attended to this responsibility with scarcely any need for special statutes that address themselves to foreign banking institutions.[2] Most of the banking laws and administrative processes in New York are applied to domestic and foreign banks alike. In the discussion which follows we concern ourselves with five areas of regulatory jurisdiction, namely *de novo* operations, capital requirements, lending restrictions, deposit functions, and examinations and related supervisory powers.

De Novo Operations

Chartering procedures and requirements for a bank, trust company, or investment company are similar to those required for all domestic commercial banks. Licenses for agencies and branches are issued by the Superintendent of Banks, with the approval of the Banking Board, for a period of up to one year. State law requires that a foreign banking corporation that maintains a branch office in New York must deposit with the Superintendent specified assets in amounts determined by the Superintendent. In the past all New York branches have deposited assets equal to 5 per cent of total liabilities.

Banking law in New York State also requires that reciprocity be available in the home country of the foreign bank. A foreign bank may be licensed to maintain a branch in New York only if the laws of its native country permit a New York

State chartered bank or trust company to maintain either a branch or agency in that country, or be authorised to own the shares of a banking organisation formed under the laws of that country.

The banking law in New York sets down the criteria and information that the Superintendent must use in approving requests for licensing and chartering. These include the character and responsibility of the persons who will conduct the business, the needs of the public, financial statements and credit reports, the views of various federal authorities including the Department of State, competence of management, facilitation of trade and commerce between the U.S. and home country of the foreign bank, competitive effects, and sources of new business of the proposed bank or banking office.

Capital Requirements

New York banking law establishes minimum amounts of capital stock in the formation of banks and trust companies, which vary with the population of the area where the bank is located. Capital requirements are more usually related to the scope of operations rather than statutory minima, and Banking Department policy generally calls for substantially larger amounts of initial capital funds before a charter application would be considered.

A foreign banking corporation wishing to obtain a branch or agency license must have assets of at least $1 million more than liabilities. This requirement parallels another section of the banking law that requires a state chartered bank have capital and surplus of $1 million before it can establish branches in foreign countries. Again, these are statutory minima and in practice the amounts of capital stock of foreign banks generally far exceeds this figure.

The New York branches of foreign banks must meet a requirement that is synonymous with a capital requirement. A branch licensee must hold in New York specified types of assets equal to at least 108 per cent of aggregate liabilities payable at or through the New York branch. In effect, every branch must maintain a capital protection whereby assets exceed deposits and other liabilities by 8 per cent of their total.[3]

There are no specific capital requirements for an agency of a foreign bank. However, in the event of liquidation of either an agency or a branch by the Superintendent the claims of creditors arising from transactions held by them directly with the licensee are to be preferred. Therefore the assets of the agency or branch are held primarily for the protection of the creditors of the New York offices.[4]

Lending Restrictions
In New York all banks and trust companies, and branches of foreign banks are subject to the same size restrictions on individual loans. Investment companies and agencies of foreign banks are not subject to restrictions on either the type or size of loans they grant.

A bank or trust company may lend unlimited amounts to the U.S. government, New York State, or other departments, agencies, or instrumentalities. Loans secured by cash collateral or securities of the above-mentioned governmental units are also exempt from lending restrictions.

Another category of loans is subject to a limit of twenty-five per cent of the bank's capital stock, surplus and undivided profits. This category includes loans to states other than New York, to foreign nations, and to quasi-utility type corporations. Loans connected with the creation of bankers' acceptances or with respect to bills of exchange are similarly limited. Unsecured loans and all other extensions of credit to an individual borrower not falling under the above provisions may not exceed ten per cent of the bank's capital base.

A separate limitation applies to loans on letters of credit and acceptance financing, which is ten per cent of capital if the acceptance is not accompanied by documents and twenty-five per cent if secured (by documents). Statutory rates of interest that may be charged on loans are identical for foreign branch offices, and banks and trust companies.

Deposit Functions
New York banking law prohibits the acceptance of deposits by any business entities except banks, trust companies, and New York branches of foreign banks. Agencies and investment companies of foreign banks are prohibited from accepting deposits, although they may maintain 'credit balances' or 'current

accounts'. These represent funds held by the investment company or agency which arise from the regular exercise of activities.[5] New York branches of foreign banks and state chartered banks and trust companies must maintain the same level of reserves against deposits as do member banks of the Federal Reserve System. Agencies and investment companies do not accept deposits, and therefore are exempt from reserve requirements.

Supervisory Powers

To assure a sound banking system and to adequately protect creditors of agencies and branches the banking law imposes minimum asset requirements relative to liabilities. A New York branch must maintain acceptable assets equal to at least 108 per cent of branch liabilities. Generally these branches maintain higher coverage ratios than this minimum. In addition, as a matter of administrative policy agencies must maintain a minimum 100 per cent coverage ratio.

The problem of qualification of assets (to satisfy these coverage ratios) is a difficult one in the case of supervising agencies and branches. Banking law disallows the following in maintaining coverage ratios:

1. Amounts due from parent bank head office, and other entities of the foreign parent bank.
2. Assets not held in New York.
3. Balances due from banks, denominated in foreign currencies which are not freely convertible into U.S. funds.

The 'New York Asset' concept is a matter of constant review and attention by the State Banking Department.[6]

The State Banking Department has available to it a number of supervisory powers, including examinations and examination reports, supervisory letters based on examination reports, moral suasion, reports of condition, and directors' examinations. The examination report assures compliance with legislative policy and reflects management effectiveness. The typical examination report covers examiner's comments relating to the condition of the institution, a statement of assets and liabilities as found by the examiner, a summary of the examination highlights, information concerning the quality and diversification of the investment portfolio, a listing of assets criticised by the examiner, a review of the foreign exchange position, the examiner's comments and suggestions on operating procedures and internal controls.

Based on the preceding summary, the writer is of the opinion that the New York State Banking Department is in a position to administer the banking laws and supervise foreign banks in a reasonably effective manner. A rapid expansion has taken place in foreign banking operations in New York. Nevertheless, there is no evidence of weakness or deterioration in quality standards.

2. OTHER STATES

In this section we examine the regulatory system as it applies to foreign banks in three states. These states have been selected because of their importance (actual or potential) as host states, and because they present interesting contrasts in approach.

California ranks second in importance as a headquarters location for foreign banks doing business in the United States. Its attraction to foreign banks is based on the large land area it encompasses, the growth in population, the opportunities for state-wide branching, and the commercial and investment ties of California with Pacific Basin countries.

The policy of California toward foreign banks has been liberal, evidenced by the large number of foreign banks operating there, and the diversity of types. California permits foreign banks to establish state chartered subsidiaries which enjoy the same privileges and responsibilities as domestically owned banking corporations. In addition, California banking law provides for the licensing of agencies and branches. Up to the present the California banking law has required that operation of a branch by a foreign bank be permitted only on the condition that Federal Deposit Insurance Corporation coverage apply to deposits in that branch. An exception permits taking foreign source deposits not protected by FDIC insurance. Since by law deposits in branches of foreign banks are not eligible for FDIC insurance coverage, branch operations in California have been precluded.

California banking law permits the merger or acquisition of domestic banks and foreign banks. In 1973 the State

Superintendent of Banks approved the acquisition of the First Western Bank & Trust Co. by Lloyds Bank Ltd., a British bank.[7] In 1974 the California Superintendent and FDIC approved the acquisition of Liberty National Bank by The Chartered Bank of London, a state chartered subsidiary of the British bank with the same name. Early in 1974 it was reported that Barclays Bank of California was in the process of acquiring the County Bank of Santa Barbara. At the same time it was reported that Baron Edmond de Rothschild of France was in the process of purchasing 600,000 shares of BanCal Tri-State Corporation, owner of the Bank of California, the state's seventh largest bank.[8] In 1975 it was reported that the Bank of Tokyo of California and the Southern California First National Bank were discussing a merger, whereby the Japanese owned institution would purchase the stock of SCFN at a price substantially higher than current market value. The San Diego based SCFN had been a subject of merger rumours on several occasions, in part due to high loan losses and a rapid changeover of top management personnel in the past three years.[9]

Illinois probably ranks as the third most important headquarters state for foreign banks. Until 1973 foreign banks were able to establish state chartered subsidiaries and representative offices in Illinois. However, they could not open branch offices in that state. In October 1973 a foreign branching law was enacted (titled the Foreign Office Banking Act), making it possible for foreign banks to establish a single branch office in the Chicago Loop area. The measure contains a reciprocity clause for Illinois banks which seek to branch overseas.[10]

The Foreign Office Banking Act was a somewhat controversial measure inasmuch as Illinois is a unit banking state. Domestic banks cannot establish branch offices in Illinois (but can establish non-U.S. offices). The smaller state chartered banks and the non-bank financial institutions objected to passage of the foreign branching law, and in 1973 a split developed in the Illinois State Banking Association over the question of branching privileges for domestic and foreign banking corporations.

Florida represents an interesting contrast to California and Illinois. Florida enjoys high per capita income and rapid economic growth. The unit banking provision in the Florida banking laws has provided significant opportunities for holding company expansion, and would provide similar opportunities for foreign bank entry into the state. In September 1972 the Royal Trust Company of Montreal, Canada acquired the Inter National Bank of Miami, a $48 million deposit institution. After the Federal Reserve Board approved the acquisition the Florida Commissioner of Banking unsuccessfully attempted to block the purchase.

Prior to the acquisition by the Canadian trust company, the Florida legislature had passed an amendment to the Banking Act which prohibited the acquisition of Florida trust companies by out of state banks, trust companies, and holding companies. The Florida statute does not apply to out of state institutions that owned or controlled a Florida bank or trust company on the date the law became effective (December 21, 1972).

In October 1974 the Royal Trust Company of Montreal announced an agreement to acquire the $2.9 million deposit American Bank of Lakeland, Florida. The agreement places a value of $2.3 million on the Lakeland bank. Royal Trust indicated it plans to continue operating the bank with its current directors, officers and personnel.

3. FEDERAL SUPERVISION

In general federal law has remained silent on the matter of foreign bank operations in the United States. Federal supervision operates uniformly vis-à-vis domestic and foreign banking entities.

Existing federal law provides for supervision of foreign banks by three federal agencies. The Federal Reserve Board has jurisdiction over BHCs which includes foreign banks that own and operate subsidiary banks in the U.S. In addition the Federal Reserve Board enforces the provisions of the Glass Steagall Act in cases of banks subject to Federal Reserve jurisdiction. The FDIC has supervisory jurisdiction over insured banks, and all state chartered banking institutions owned by foreign banks have FDIC protection. This includes FDIC authority to conduct examinations. The FDIC also must approve mergers of insured banks, and in 1974 under this authority decided in favour of the acquisition of the Liberty National Bank by The

Chartered Bank of London. Finally, the Comptroller of the Currency has regular supervisory authority over the national banks including the power to examine and report on the condition and status of national banks.

With the 1970 amendment to the Bank Holding Company Act, important ground rules came into being with respect to all BHC acquisitions. Prior to the 1970 amendment the BHC Act applied only in cases of multi-bank holding companies. Until that time foreign banks and nonbank investors especially were operating in the dark and could not be certain that federal authorities would remain neutral in specific cases of bank acquisitions. Moreover, there was always the possibility of Department of Justice determination that such acquisitions violated the antitrust provisions of the Bank Merger Act.

The 1970 amendment provided clear and definite jurisdiction by the Board of Governors over national and state banks. Moreover, it provided for a formal administrative procedure for holding company acquisitions of U.S. banks. The Board of Governors renders administrative rulings, subject to review and possible modification based upon submission of further evidence.

The 1970 amendment covers the area of non-banking acquisitions. Bank holding companies are able to plan and implement acquisitions of nonbank companies in areas of finance that are considered complementary to commercial banking. Foreign banks have found the holding company structure a useful and flexible approach that satisfies their needs and requirements in the United States.

The final element in the regulatory framework facing foreign banks is the Glass Steagall Act. In Congressional testimony preceding passage of the Act, legislators indicated that affiliation between commercial banks and securities companies can lead to potential conflicts of interest and unsound banking practices. American bankers have been permitted to depart from the strict separation of commercial and investment banking only under carefully delimited circumstances and within narrowly specified areas. These include bank underwriting of government securities and international banking affiliate activities (Edge Act subsidiaries of U.S. banks). More recently U.S. banks have been permitted to provide monthly investment services to stock market investors on a retail basis.

Foreign banking systems differ considerably from the U.S. model, and in other countries it is possible for commercial banks to engage in securities brokerage and underwriting. Federal regulatory authorities with supervisory jurisdiction over foreign banks have attempted to maintain a separation between commercial and investment banking activities of foreign banks in the United States. In one case an Italian bank, Banco di Roma, wanted to expand its representation in Chicago with a full service office. In 1972 Banco di Roma applied for and obtained permission to form a bank holding company by establishing and then acquiring 100 per cent of the shares of Banco di Roma (Chicago), a proposed new bank. The Federal Reserve Board approved this request. However, in a separate order the Board denied the request of the Italian bank as a bank holding company to retain its one-third interest in EuroPartners Securities Corporation, a New York securities brokerage firm. Since close to three-fourths of EuroPartners income was derived from foreign sources, Banco di Roma had applied for a special exemption for its investment in the securities affiliate. The Board's denial was based in part on the unfair competitive advantage a foreign bank holding company would have over a domestic bank. The Board left open the option for Banco di Roma to acquire the Chicago subsidiary, and divest ownership in EuroPartners within two years.[11]

B. ALLEGED PROBLEMS AND DEFICIENCIES

In the period 1973–75 several proposals have been made to provide for federal regulation and supervision of foreign banking activities in the United States. We consider these proposals in the following section of this chapter which deals with regulatory proposals at the federal level. In this section we examine the problems and deficiencies in the current regulatory system as viewed by Congressional and other proponents of regulatory reform. The reasons that have been offered for these regulatory proposals include the following:

1. Strengthen monetary policy.
2. Control capital flows.
3. Assure reciprocity.

4. Place domestic banks on par with foreign banks in the U.S.
  5. Prevent undesirable changes in banking structure.
  6. Provide an alternative to state chartering and open all states to foreign banking.

1. STRENGTHEN MONETARY POLICY

Governor Mitchell of the Federal Reserve Board has pointed out that international monetary flows through foreign owned banking institutions are not subject to Federal Reserve jurisdiction. In June 1973 the Federal Reserve Board requested foreign banks operating in the United States to conform voluntarily to marginal reserve requirements imposed on large certificates of deposit and net Eurodollar borrowings.

A clear distinction should be made between federal regulation in the two areas of monetary policy and supervision of bank operations and banking structure. Need for supervisory authority over licensing, chartering, and operations must be justified on its own merits. Application of reserve requirements by the Federal Reserve Board can be defended if foreign bank operations in the U.S. are sufficiently large to present a significant gap in coverage and if state imposed reserve requirements are inadequate. It seems clear that there may be greater need to extend uniform reserve requirements on all domestic banks including nonmember banks, than on foreign banks operating in the U.S. At yearend 1974 assets of nonmember banks were nearly four times the amount of assets held by foreign banking institutions. In fact, close to one-third of foreign bank resources would be covered if all state chartered nonmember banks (including foreign owned) were made subject to uniform reserve requirements.

2. CONTROL CAPITAL FLOWS

Foreign bank branches and agencies in the United States are direct operating arms of their parent institutions. Consequently, their basic rationale for existence will be to make loans to non-residents and to accept deposits from offshore areas. Moreover, these U.S. located offices will participate in foreign exchange transactions, manage the money market investments of parent institutions, and engage in other transactions giving rise to capital inflows and outflows. The United States derives considerable financial service income, domestic income generation, and financial expertise and leadership as a result of these activities. These foreign banking offices represent important conduits through which large scale international money flows take place. Balance of payments considerations alone might warrant consideration of means by which regulatory authorities can monitor foreign bank transactions that give rise to inflows and outflows of capital. On the other hand, it can be held that the international divisions of large American banks are equally responsible for initiating capital flows. No proposals have been forthcoming to monitor or regulate their transactions, and the January 1974 removal of foreign lending restraints may be viewed as a move in the opposite direction.

The closer alignment of the U.S. prime rate with the London interbank rate on Eurodollars suggests that U.S. domestic banks can enjoy greater flexibility in competing for and participating in international credit market activities. Finally, we should note that other countries are far more exposed to international flows of liquid funds than the United States, and remain able to apply suitable general monetary restraint as well as specific restraint measures against capital flow influences on domestic liquidity.

3. ASSURE RECIPROCITY

The question of insuring that American banks obtain reciprocal favourable treatment from foreign governments has been battered about for close to a decade. It is difficult to argue that American banks have been heavily or arbitrarily discriminated against, especially if we examine in a detailed fashion the pattern and gross magnitudes of American bank expansion abroad. Admittedly, several important countries exclude direct U.S. banking representation (Australia, Canada, and the Scandinavian countries). But these are exceptions.

The New York statute (1960) permitting foreign bank branches contains a reciprocity provision. It has been argued that domestic banks are handicapped when their respective states do not grant reciprocity to foreign banks. While this has not been visibly demonstrated, there may be specific instances where such a problem exists. However, the major international banking states permit foreign bank representation and we must assume that the American banks headquartered in these states are relatively free to obtain access to offshore banking facilities.

The definition or interpretation of reciprocity remains a clouded issue. Foreign banks argue that an interpretation based on permitting foreign banks to conduct business according to the guidelines operating vis-à-vis domestic banks is overly restrictive. This is because U.S. bank regulation tends to be more control oriented than in other countries. American banks operating in foreign countries are afforded far more leeway than at home, and therefore it is argued obtain more advantages than foreign banks operating in the U.S. For example, in 1973 when the New York State Superintendent of Banks denied the Barclays Bank request to acquire the Long Island Trust Company on the basis of competitive effects (a First National City Bank or Chase Manhattan acquisition also would have been denied), foreign banks felt that application of U.S. standards represented an interpretation of reciprocity that was harmful to them.

The extension of supervisory jurisdiction over foreign banks to federal authorities can be argued for in terms of achieving a more uniform set of standards applicable to foreign banks, and in terms of centralising bargaining power to achieve increased reciprocal treatment for American banks. However, it has not been established that denial of reciprocal treatment has been damaging to the overseas activities of American banks. More important, it is doubtful that such centralisation of supervisory powers would induce foreign governments to open their doors to foreign (and U.S.) banks. Australia and Canada appear to be adopting harder positions vis-à-vis foreign ownership of strategic industry sectors such as banking. American banks have obtained representation in these markets via 'near banking' affiliates, which may be all that can reasonably be expected.

4. PLACE DOMESTIC BANKS ON PAR WITH FOREIGN BANKS IN U.S.

American critics have argued that foreign banks enjoy several advantages over U.S. banks in their operations in this country. This relates to the lower cost of operations (FDIC insurance and reserve requirements), ability to engage in certain investment banking activities, and greater freedom to operate on an interstate basis.

In practice, New York branches of foreign banks must conform to the same percentage reserve requirements and loan limitations as state chartered banks. Moreover, a 1969 amendment to the banking law requires that branches and agencies of foreign banks in New York maintain assets equivalent to 108 per cent of liabilities. State chartered affiliates of foreign banks have obtained FDIC insurance coverage, and only *branches* of foreign banks enjoy cost advantages in this area. A major source of cost advantage lies in cases where state reserve requirements are lower than those of the Federal Reserve. We have seen in a previous chapter that this is not a significant factor in states such as New York and California where the heaviest concentration of foreign banking is located.

As a practical matter foreign banks are not important factors in the securities or investment banking areas in the United States. Several large Swiss and German banks simultaneously operate New York branches and securities affiliates. However, where BHC jurisdiction applies the Board of Governors has effectively sought to maintain the separation of investment from deposit banking. The few minor exceptions of foreign bank activity in investment banking do not appear significant enough to justify any special extension of federal jurisdiction. Moreover, it could be argued that these exceptions make it feasible for inward portfolio investment that has operated to strengthen the U.S. balance of payments.

Finally, interstate operations of foreign banks in the U.S. have tended to cause concern over the possibility of unfair competitive advantages. We should note that there are two aspects of these interstate activities. First, some part of this parallels the interstate activities of U.S. banks that enjoy multiple Edge Act affiliate representation in several international banking subcentres (New York, San Francisco, Los Angeles, Chicago, Houston, Boston, and Miami). In such cases it is not possible to assert that foreign banks enjoy clearcut competitive advantages.[12] As a matter of fact, American banks with Edge Act affiliates may be able to operate more flexibly in areas such as specialty financing. Second, some part of foreign bank interstate representation may involve a mix of retail-wholesale banking not directly associated with international finance. In such cases a competitive advantage accrues to the foreign bank. Whether this competitive advantage is sufficient to justify special federal jurisdiction remains an open question. Recent legislative proposals by the New York Superintendent of Banks for reciprocal interstate banking privileges (with California and other states) appear to offer a flexible solution, that would result in minimal interference with state prerogatives over bank legislation. Federal regulators and the U.S. Congress might well look in this direction, since it represents a liberalising rather than restrictive approach. It seems appropriate to place greater priority in the direction of regulatory reforms that liberalise the treatment accorded domestic banks rather than on measures that cut foreign bank activities down to the lowest common denominator of American regulatory practices.

5. PREVENT UNDESIRABLE CHANGES IN BANKING STRUCTURE

It has been argued that foreign banking activities operate as a stimulus for change in U.S. banking structure. The areas of change include interstate banking operations, and extension of bank holding company activities to near banking areas.

Consideration should be given to the need for such changes. If changes in American banking structure are needed these needs should be examined and lawmakers should address themselves to the best approach. In the previous section reference was made to reciprocal interstate banking. There are very strong arguments for moving in this direction. It would be tragic if federal legislative reforms came that inhibited development of reciprocal interstate banking privileges.

6. PROVIDE AN ALTERNATIVE TO STATE CHARTERING AND OPEN ALL STATES TO FOREIGN BANKING

The argument for extending federal regulatory authority over foreign banks is based in part on the need to provide an alternative to state chartering, and to open all states to foreign banking. The second half of the preceding statement does not rest on firm ground, since it is unlikely that sufficient international banking business exists in more than ten or twelve states to justify a foreign banking presence. Operation of foreign banking facilities in the remaining forty states would be uneconomic.

Alternatives to state chartering do exist. Foreign banks have acquired majority or complete ownership of state and national banks under the provisions of the BHC Act. Moreover, foreign banks have not properly explored the feasibility of obtaining Federal Reserve membership for their state chartered banking affiliates, and establishing Edge Act affiliates in other states, as do domestically owned member banks. Such options may be available, and deserve consideration by all concerned.

C. REGULATORY PROPOSALS AT THE FEDERAL LEVEL

In the period 1973–75 there has been a flurry of discussion and proposals to extend federal jurisdiction over foreign banking activities. This situation almost parallels that which followed demise of the Intra Bank, and the concern over protecting U.S. depositors who had placed funds in the New York branch of that Lebanese institution. Fortunately, the current interest in foreign banking in the United States does not stem as much from foreign bank failures as it does from the successful growth of their operations in this country. Added to these pressures is a moderately intensified protectionist viewpoint that has emerged in the United States in the wake of the 1971 and 1973 dollar devaluations, the low level of stock market prices which invite takeover bids, and the sustained weakness in the U.S. balance of payments position.

During 1973 two legislative proposals were filed in the U.S. Congress that would affect foreign banking operations in the United States, the Patman and Rees bills. In 1974 the Board of Governors of the Federal Reserve System made public its own legislative proposal, which was resubmitted to Congress in 1975. Considerable discussion has developed as a result of these regulatory proposals. The Federal Reserve authorities circulated their proposal among foreign central banks for comment, and other interested parties have made public their views in these areas. The viewpoints expressed by interested parties is reflected in Section D.

1. THE PATMAN BILL

The Patman Bill, known as the Foreign Bank Control Act, was introduced in Congress originally in November 1973. Several considerations appear to have served as motivation for this bill.

These include the advantages allegedly possessed by foreign banks over U.S. banking institutions, the monetary policy implications of foreign bank growth, and the need to preserve the competitive structure in American banking markets.

The bill provides that foreign banks apply to the Secretary of the Treasury for permission to establish or continue operations in the United States. Upon approval, final authority to charter the foreign bank would rest with the appropriate banking authority. This would be the Board of Governors of the Federal Reserve System in the case of federally chartered subsidiaries engaged in international banking, and the Federal Deposit Insurance Corporation and State Banking Superintendent in the case of subsidiaries engaged in domestic banking. There would be no alternative to this procedure for licensing of foreign banking operations.

All banking operations by foreign banks in the U.S. would be conducted through subsidiaries, rather than through a combination of subsidiaries, branches and agencies as is currently the procedure. A foreign bank would be limited to one domestic banking subsidiary (state chartered) whose activities would be limited to a single state. Foreign banks would continue to be excluded from states which have laws specifically forbidding foreign banking. Individual foreign banks would be limited to five federally chartered international banking subsidiaries, which could operate in more than one state as domestic banks do through their Edge Act subsidiaries. In this connection the bill incorporates much of the language contained in the Edge Act (Section 25a of the Federal Reserve Act), and restricts the federally chartered banking subsidiaries to international activities. This approximates the activity now permitted agencies of foreign banks in New York and California.

The bill prohibits establishment of overseas branches and subsidiaries by foreign owned banks based in the United States. This would deny federally chartered subsidiaries that operate in a manner similar to Edge Act affiliates certain powers that Edge affiliates find most advantageous. This is the authority to establish overseas branches and to make equity investments overseas.

Foreign owned banks would be required to adhere to Federal Reserve reserve requirements, in amount and composition.

Moreover, under this proposal the Board could impose additional reserve requirements on subsidiaries of foreign banks with federal charters. Foreign bank subsidiaries would not be eligible for membership in the Federal Reserve System.

Mergers between foreign bank subsidiaries and domestic American banks would be prohibited.[13] There would be no grandfather protection of non-conforming activities (securities affiliates and interstate offices).

The Patman Bill generally has been considered somewhat restrictive in its treatment of foreign banks. In some circles it has been regarded as harsh enough to generate a reaction outside the United States that would be counter-productive to the general intent of the bill. The overly restrictive attitude toward foreign bank operations and failure to treat foreign banks on a par with domestic banks represent major weaknesses in the Patman Bill.

In the areas of equality of treatment, the Patman Bill treats foreign banks in a discriminatory fashion as compared with domestic banks. First, foreign banks would be precluded from obtaining national bank charters to conduct domestic operations in the United States. Second, only one domestic banking subsidiary would be allowed in a state. Domestic banks may be part of a multi-bank holding company within a state. Third, mergers or consolidations of foreign bank subsidiaries with domestic banks would be prohibited. Fourth, foreign bank subsidiaries would be barred from Federal Reserve membership, and all of the privileges of such membership. Fifth, a foreign bank would be limited to five international banking subsidiaries in the United States whereas there is no statutory limit on the number of Edge affiliates a member bank of the Federal Reserve may operate. Sixth, an international banking subsidiary of a foreign bank would not be permitted to have foreign branches or make foreign equity investments. Edge corporations of domestic banks may carry out these activities.

Finally, we should note that the Patman Bill provides for a rather complicated distribution of supervisory authority. The Federal Reserve, FDIC, and State Banking Superintendent would be involved in chartering foreign bank subsidiaries, while the Comptroller of the Currency would have authority to conduct examinations. In short, there would be at least as many agencies with supervisory jurisdiction as we currently have. This arrangement appears to be unnecessarily complicated.

2. THE REES BILL

The Rees Bill was submitted to Congress shortly after the Patman Bill. The Rees Bill is basically similar to the earlier proposal. In fact, there are only a few minor differences, which are described below.

The Rees Bill would prohibit the establishment of branches by a state chartered subsidiary of a foreign bank in a state other than that in which the subsidiary is located. However, it would make exceptions in situations where the state law that has primary jurisdiction over that subsidiary specifically authorises establishment of a branch in another state. Most probably, this provision in the Rees Bill is designed to accommodate legislation proposed in the California and New York state legislatures permitting reciprocal branching.

A second difference is that the Rees Bill adds a provision relating to the operations of foreign branches of American banks. The provision authorises the Board of Governors to limit the amount of any or all classes of liabilities or assets held by any foreign branch, and to prescribe any reserve ratio against all classes of liabilities held by any branch, whenever necessary for the conduct of monetary policy. This particular item does not appear to be closely connected with the scope of activities of foreign banks in the United States.

3. FEDERAL RESERVE PROPOSAL

The Federal Reserve Proposal was the outgrowth of the work of the System Steering Committee on International Banking Regulation which the Board established in 1973. Two general objectives appear to have shaped the Federal Reserve proposal, namely to achieve equality of treatment in the regulation and supervision of foreign and domestic banks operating in the United States and to bring foreign banks within the control of the central bank in order to promote the effectiveness of monetary policy.

The Federal Reserve proposal would make all foreign banks operating branches, agencies and subsidiaries in the United

States holding companies under the Bank Holding Company Act.[14] It would further provide for a federal alternative to state chartering and licensing. The authority for federal chartering and licensing would be vested with the Comptroller of the Currency. All foreign bank entities in the United States would be covered by FDIC insurance, and all such entities would be members of the Federal Reserve System. Moreover, foreign banks would be permitted to own Edge corporations.

Under the Federal Reserve proposal foreign banks would be limited in their domestic (U.S.) banking operations to a single state, but could expand their operations within that state on the same terms and conditions as domestic banks. Moreover, foreign banks would be able to operate nonbanking subsidiaries throughout the United States in the same manner as domestic bank holding companies. However, ownership of securities affiliates would be precluded to foreign banks operating U.S. banking offices.

The Federal Reserve proposal opens up opportunities for the chartering of national banks by foreigners. Power of approval would lie within the office of the Comptroller, and the requirements relating to U.S. citizenship of all directors would be modified. This provides an alternative to state chartering. In addition it makes it possible for foreign banks to operate in states closed to them under existing state statutes.

The proposal would require that all foreign owned banking units in the United States be members of the Federal Reserve System where the foreign bank involved has worldwide assets in excess of $500 million. The Federal Reserve Board has maintained that, with minor exceptions, foreign banks operating in the United States are all large banks and therefore in direct competition with the largest of U.S. banks. Membership in the Federal Reserve System would oblige foreign banking entities in the United States to conform to reserve requirements in the same manner as domestic member banks, and provide them access to the discount window facilities and other services of the Fed. In this manner central bank monetary policy would be strengthened and foreign bank advantages in the way of lower effective reserve requirements would be removed.

The proposal would require that all foreign bank entities

obtain FDIC insurance on deposit liabilities. At present subsidiary banks of foreign banking institutions are required to carry FDIC insurance, but branches of foreign banks in the U.S. are not eligible for this insurance. The requirement of deposit insurance would remove a small cost advantage enjoyed by foreign banks, and place these banks on a more competitively equal footing with domestic banks in attracting deposits.

The Federal Reserve further proposes that foreign banks be permitted to own Edge Act corporations, or be permitted to operate with equivalent entities. This would permit foreign banks to establish subsidiaries in major international banking centres across the United States, providing a more equal competitive status for foreign banks as compared with domestic banking institutions.

Finally, the Federal Reserve proposal would restrict non-conforming activities. This includes stock brokerage, underwriting and interstate operations. Several grandfathering options would be considered including permission to continue non-conforming services for non-U.S. customers, or limiting future expansion of domestic banking to one state while retaining existing offices in other states.

The Federal Reserve proposal appears to be relatively moderate, especially when compared with the Patman and Rees proposals. Foreign banking institutions are placed on a competitive par with domestic banks, and are authorised to operate as flexibly as American banks.

D. INSTITUTIONAL PRESSURES

The eightfold growth of foreign bank assets in the United States in the period 1965–74 has given rise to increasing institutional pressures. These tensions are reflected in the relationships between state and federal banking authorities, between state banking authorities and domestic commercial banks, between foreign and domestic banks, and between different categories of domestic banks and financial institutions. The following discussion focuses on the issues around which these various conflicts have developed. Any effort at modifying the regulatory treatment of foreign banks in the United States will affect these relationships in a variety of ways. Moreover, as the following discussion points out, it is virtually impossible to isolate or narrow down the focus of issues because of their complex interrelations.

1. STATE AND FEDERAL BANKING AUTHORITIES

While the dual banking system in the U.S. has operated for over a century, foreign banks have relied mainly on the states to obtain chartering and licensing privileges. Only in recent years have foreign banks become subject to federal supervision under the Bank Holding Company Act. For various reasons Congress has not seen it appropriate to create federal supervisory authority in this area.

The resulting regulatory structure has created numerous problems in the relationships between state and federal banking authorities. First, foreign banks operating in the U.S. are subject to state laws which are different from state to state. These different state laws are influenced by local interests, and may not reflect a common national viewpoint. The Federal Reserve Board of Governors does not have effective control over the credit supplied by state chartered foreign banking subsidiaries, branches and agencies. This has been expressed at the federal level as a serious deficiency in the conduct of monetary policy. All three regulatory proposals discussed in this chapter would make foreign banks subject to Federal Reserve jurisdiction in matters relating to monetary policy.

Another area of developing institutional conflict between state and federal agencies focuses on the wider latitude afforded foreign banks in conducting inter-state business. Several large foreign banks operate agencies, branches and subsidiaries in more than one state. With exceptions discussed previously, domestic banks are prohibited from engaging in banking activities from offices located in more than one state. The Federal Reserve has attempted to live with the prohibitions against interstate representation of domestic banks. Moreover, the Federal Reserve has suggested that in fairness to domestic banks, foreign banking operations should be brought into conformity with those of domestic banks that are prevented from extending market areas across state boundaries. To restrict foreign banks to doing business in one state only has been opposed on the ground that foreign countries may retaliate against U.S. banks operating in their countries. Many states feel it is not necessary for federal authorities to step into what has been a long-established area of state jurisdiction, especially since foreign banking operations are relatively small in most states. Several states may be willing to grant foreign banks permission to establish branches in their jurisdiction but hesitate to do so as long as foreign branches are not considered eligible for federal deposit insurance.

2. STATE BANKING AUTHORITIES AND DOMESTIC BANKS

Growth of foreign banking in the U.S. has introduced anomalous situations in states where these institutions are heavily represented. In some cases domestic banks have demanded equal treatment in such areas as branching privileges (interstate and intrastate).

States may be divided into three categories where branching provisions are concerned. These include:

1. State-wide branching permitted. This includes several important foreign banking states (California, Arizona, Washington, New Jersey, and Connecticut).
2. Limited branching permitted. This includes two states that have foreign bank representation (New York, Massachusetts, Michigan, New Mexico, and Louisiana).
3. Unit banking states. These states permit no branching (Illinois, Florida, Texas, and Missouri).

A growing presence of foreign banks has created major problems between the various state banking authorities and U.S. domestic banks. Two difficulties emerge with respect to branching provisions. Differences in state laws make it possible for foreign banking corporations to expand more rapidly than competing domestic banks fenced in by unit banking or limited branching laws. Foreign banks can select states for entry into the U.S. that permit branching. Moreover, they can use the branch form in additional states and most especially in unit banking states where the subsidiary form is less attractive.

American banks complain about unfair treatment they receive from states which permit state-wide banking for foreign banks, but not to domestic banks domiciled in other states. Unit banking states such as Illinois have permitted foreign banks to establish a single branch but continue to prohibit within-state branching by domestic banks domiciled in that state. While it is true that Edge Act units of domestic banks can operate in states other than that of their parent institution, they are prohibited from conducting any domestic business. Given these conditions, foreign banks can take advantage of varying state laws and establish different types of organisational units in different states to carry on a mixture of local, national and international business, while domestic banks cannot compete with them on the same basis.

The California and New York Superintendents of Banking have endorsed bills introduced in their respective legislatures which provide for reciprocal branching privileges. These proposals would permit New York banks to establish a limited number of branch offices in California, and would grant the same privileges to California banks in New York State. Enactment of these bills would permit domestic banks to compete in a more flexible manner with the expansion of foreign banking in the United States, and more important to operate in the *two* regional banking markets that have proven the most fruitful for foreign banking institutions.

3. FEDERAL AUTHORITIES AND FOREIGN BANKS

Institutional pressures arise whenever foreign banks establish direct representation in a host country. These conflicts are heightened or intensified when there are substantial differences in banking structure and bank operations between the home country of the foreign bank and the host country. Moreover, these differences complicate the granting of reciprocal banking privileges to foreign banking institutions.

Differences in banking structure and operations that appear to present especially difficult problems for U.S. policy makers include the dual levels at which bank chartering takes place, the wide differences in branching laws between the states, and the narrower conception of bank operations as codified in national banking legislation. For example in many countries foreign banks are not prohibited from engaging in investment banking activities, and consider membership on the stock exchanges, underwriting of corporate securities, and securities brokerage activities as a normal adjunct of the bank's deposit and loan operations. Finally, the American propensity to attack monopoly in banking tends to leave a wide gulf between what is considered reasonable practices and undue control of the credit markets.

The development of overseas banking by American banks and the increasing penetration of U.S. credit and loan markets by foreign banks has been possible because of the reciprocity relationships developed and adhered to by the regulatory agencies possessing jurisdiction. Many questions have been raised in recent years regarding the extension of reciprocity privileges. Should the U.S. permit foreign banking if the home country of the foreign bank denies the same treatment to U.S. banks? Canada, the Scandinavian countries and Australia are cases in point.

A more fundamental problem hinges on the specific meaning of reciprocity. Does it mean that foreign banks should be permitted to conduct banking as they do at home, or according to the banking regulations in the U.S.? Should the standard of reciprocity be state-wide, or country-wide? Should some or all banking practices of the foreign country or the host country be determining in terms of the scope of activities of the foreign bank? In this instance large Chicago banks that do business abroad could be hurt because they could no longer have the leverage of reciprocity (Illinois is a unit banking state which confines foreign banks operating in that state to a single banking office). If foreign banks are accorded the same treatment as U.S. domestic banks under the dual chartering system foreign banks would ordinarily prefer state chartered subsidiaries with FDIC deposit protection, but without Federal Reserve membership.

Special problems emerge when we consider that several foreign banks operate securities affiliates in the United States, which seems to be contrary to the intent of the Banking Act of 1933. These banks have not fallen under the jurisdiction of the Federal Reserve Board as BHCs, and therefore the question of reciprocity at the federal level has been deferred. In another connection foreign bank acquisitions of domestic banks may not be permitted due to the application of U.S. standards regarding competitive effects. Application of this standard resulted in a negative decision when a British bank requested permission to acquire a large Long Island bank in 1973. This decision led European bankers to question the U.S. interpretation of reciprocity, inasmuch as American banking and business interests in several European countries have grown to absorb a large share of the market.[15]

4. CONFLICT OVER FOREIGN BANKS AND FOREIGN CAPITAL

Over the period 1960–75 the U.S. government has encouraged foreign investment inflows. Investment inflows have increased at an impressive pace, helping to strengthen the U.S. balance of payments. Foreign investors generally prefer to make use of the banking facilities of their own country. To better service home country business firms and investors foreign banks prefer to conduct a full range of banking and financial services. In this connection they regard it as essential that they be permitted to function as underwriters and securities brokers and dealers.

At present, a number of foreign banks own and operate securities affiliates in the United States. Nevertheless, they face increasing institutional rigidities. A major obstacle has been the Glass Steagall Act, but increasingly domestic banks and securities firms complain about unfair competitive advantage. In a significant case that was decided in 1973 the Federal Reserve Board denied the request of a foreign bank holding company to retain a one-third interest in a New York securities affiliate and at the same time establish a Chicago subsidiary bank.

Whereas the U.S. welcomes foreign business and portfolio investment, the provisions of the Glass Steagall Act and other banking laws restrict the development of foreign banking. Foreign banks subject to the BHC Act must conform to Federal Reserve Board rulings which work toward enforcement of Glass Steagall. Thus far foreign banks operating securities affiliates in the U.S. have escaped BHC status by utilising branches rather than state chartered subsidiaries. Many of the states which have benefited from foreign manufacturing investment have maintained a strictly exclusive policy toward the licensing or chartering of foreign banks. Inevitably, foreign banks must complain that the United States welcomes foreign investment capital but not foreign banks.

5. FOREIGN AND DOMESTIC BANKS

Our discussion of institutional pressures would be incomplete if we did not address ourselves to the changing relationships between foreign and domestic banks. Complementary relationships are gradually displacing competitive relationships, and the domestic banking community in the U.S. is splitting into two separate groups—the larger more progressive banks and the smaller less flexible institutions.

In the period 1964–69 it was possible to consider the relationships between domestic and foreign banks as predominately competitive. Foreign banks represented a new force in the United States, and were busy penetrating market sectors previously monopolised by domestic banks. The Bank Holding Company Act of 1970 had not been enacted, and one-bank holding companies were still beyond the jurisdiction of the Federal Reserve Board in matters pertaining to financial policy and acquisitions. Foreign banks had not yet fully adopted the competitive strategy of patterning their global expansion along the lines of larger American banks.

In the early 1970s these clearly competitive relationships became blurred. First, American banks have become splintered into rival factions. Larger U.S. banks have become the champions of innovations that would break down previously existing barriers to new methods of competition, while the smaller banks have become increasingly more protective toward maintaining existing deposit and credit market structures. In this connection the larger U.S. institutions have become more closely aligned with the foreign banks that have direct representation in the U.S. Both types of institutions tend to be innovative, seek a wider interstate basis of operations, tend to take a global view of their market potential, and extend their operations into near-banking pursuits. Complementary relationships between large U.S. and foreign banks have further developed as reciprocity relationships have become more important to both groups. A widening base of overseas operations and a larger stake in international activities has tended to make both groups more sensitive to the need for guaranteeing reciprocal banking privileges.

While large U.S. and foreign banks have found stronger ties of complementary interests, smaller U.S. and foreign banks have found greater conflict of interest. This has resulted in scattered pressures for reactive banking legislation that might protect smaller domestic banking institutions from further competitive pressures from foreign and large U.S. banks.

E. ALTERNATIVE APPROACHES

Thus far in our discussion we have seen that there is a wide spectrum of viewpoint concerning the regulation of foreign banks in the United States. This is reflected in the legislative proposals reviewed in a previous section. The wide spectrum in points of view can be better understood by considering the development of institutional pressures regarding American banking structure, the rights and interests of different banking groups, and the degree to which the American economy should become subject to greater international competitive forces.

Points of view regarding appropriate modification of the existing regulatory schema range from a restrictive approach to more liberalised treatment of foreign banks. In the discussion which follows we examine three distinct approaches toward regulation of foreign banks in the United States. These three approaches may be characterised as (1) Restrictive Approach, (2) Equal Treatment Approach, and (3) Liberalised Approach.

1. RESTRICTIVE APPROACH

The restrictive approach would justify extending federal regulatory authority on the basis of strong competitive advantages enjoyed by foreign banks operating in the United States and the need to equalise these advantages. In part it is based on concern that joint investments among multinational banks tend to reduce competition between parent banking institutions. Finally, we should note that traces of 'populist banking' sentiment seem to favour small domestic banking institutions which allegedly are unable to respond effectively to the foreign competition.

The restrictive approach places heavy emphasis on maintaining the status quo in the United States. This would result in prohibiting interstate banking activities, restricting banks from engaging in the securities business, and treating international banking as a separate and distinct sphere of the banking business. Moreover, extension of federal regulatory authority over foreign banks would reduce their organisational flexibility by barring the use of American branches, limiting foreign banks to a small number of federally chartered international banking affiliates, and prohibiting foreign owned BHCs from acquiring substantial equity interests in near-banking corporations (e.g. finance companies, mortgage banks, computer service firms).

The restrictive approach would go far beyond narrowing down the competitive advantages of foreign banks, and would place them at a serious disadvantage vis-à-vis U.S. banks in both the domestic and international banking areas of operation. To paraphrase Chairman Arthur F. Burns of the Federal Reserve Board, these 'provisions would create inequalities between foreign banks and domestic banks in a way that might . . . invite retaliatory treatment against the operations of U.S. banks in foreign countries'.

2. EQUAL TREATMENT APPROACH

A second approach would attempt to equalise the regulatory treatment accorded foreign banks by bringing them under the control of the central bank and federal laws. This would assure conformity to monetary policy guidelines, impose the same reserve-liquidity-deposit insurance burdens as are imposed on domestic banks, and give foreign banks the same flexibility of operations as domestic institutions.

The equal treatment approach aims to accomplish its objectives by increasing the regulatory burdens that foreign banks would be exposed to, so that they might share equally with domestic banks in their responsibilities to federal agencies. Areas of extended federal regulatory coverage include required membership in the Federal Reserve, supervision by the Comptroller of the Currency in matters pertaining to issuance of charters and licenses, and required federal deposit insurance coverage.

Under this approach existing competitive advantages of foreign banks would be narrowed down by exposing them to higher costs of operation (application of Federal Reserve requirements on reserves, FDIC insurance), preventing further development of their interstate banking operations, and prohibition of ownership of securities affiliates.

On the other hand, foreign banks would be extended additional flexibility and scope of operations in areas presently enjoyed by American banks. This would include access to the Federal Reserve discount window, ability to obtain federal charters in states that do not authorise foreign banks or issue charters for branches of foreign banks, authority to establish Edge Act or similar subsidiaries throughout the United States to conduct international business in the same way and on the same terms as domestic banks, and ability to operate nonbanking subsidiaries throughout the United States in the same manner as domestic bank holding companies.

The equal treatment approach would, in fact, equalise the scope of operations between domestic and foreign banks in the United States. However, we should note that foreign banks regard the American system of bank regulation and supervision as unnecessarily burdensome. Moreover, they have pointed out that they regard the U.S. definition of reciprocity treatment as one-sided. American authorities have tended to regard reciprocity as requiring that they permit foreign banks to operate within the same constraints as U.S. banks. Foreign banks hold that their countries provide more flexible guidelines for banking operations, and therefore American banks gain more as a result of 'reciprocity' than foreign banks operating in the U.S.

3. LIBERALISED TREATMENT

A third approach would liberalise the regulatory treatment of banks operating in the United States. Underlying this approach is the belief that changing conditions warrant a review of the present structure and regulation of American banking. Ancillary arguments relate to the need to bring foreign and domestic banks into operational conformity.

This approach aims to accomplish its objectives by selectively liberalising the regulatory treatment of domestic banks so that they might more easily respond to the competitive thrust of foreign banking in the United States. In addition, some activities of foreign banks of a nonconforming nature (investment banking) would be placed under federal supervision.

The liberalised treatment accorded domestic banks could be expected to fall most prominently in the area of interstate banking operations. Legislative proposals at both the state and

REGULATORY ISSUES AND ALTERNATIVES 125

federal levels currently provide for some form of reciprocal interstate banking privileges. The New York and California Banking Superintendents both have expressed interest in this approach. If extended to a few additional important international banking states (Illinois, Massachusetts, and Texas), this measure would remove a substantial part of the competitive advantage presently enjoyed by foreign banks.

Selective extension of federal authority over foreign banks would make the liberalised treatment approach workable. This would include equalisation of reserve requirements (as to percentage level and form in which held) and deposit insurance coverage applicable to foreign banks.

This approach probably would not be antagonistic in the eyes of foreign governments and foreign banks. Moreover, it would open up the possibility of permitting the American banking structure to respond competitively to changing needs and requirements.

8 Lessons from the U.K. Experience

> That island of England breeds very valiant creatures:
> their mastiffs are of unmatchable courage.
>
> *Henry V*

A. FOREIGN BANKS IN LONDON

For over a century London has functioned as an international financial and banking centre. This status accrued to The City as a result of the far-flung colonial empire that required varied financial and banking services, the substantial accumulation of overseas investments by U.K. residents, the outstanding financial markets in the U.K., and from the role of sterling as the reserve and settlement currency of a globe-girdling political system. British investment in the regions of dependency accumulated, and added to the banking and financial ties that linked the various units of this system together. Unfortunately, the two global wars in the first half of this century seriously limited the role played by London as an international financial centre.

In the years since World War II London has regained its previous status, and moved on to develop new functional relationships as a world banking centre. As a result, foreign banking representation has expanded three-fold since 1960, numbering over 226 foreign banks in 1973.

The variety of banking-type institutions represented is not equalled in any other international centre. More important, the share of deposits and banking business enjoyed by banks in the overseas and foreign categories is extremely high. Foreign and overseas banks hold close to 20 per cent of the sterling deposits in all U.K. banks (Table 8-1) and 83 per cent of non-sterling deposits. On an overall basis this represents 58 per cent of all deposits housed in U.K. banks. The American banks hold 37 per cent of the non-sterling deposits, and 26 per cent of all deposits in the U.K.

Table 8-1

Deposit Structure in U.K. Banks 1974

	£ Billions					
	Sterling Deposits		Non-Sterling Deposits		Total Deposits	
Deposits in	£	%	£	%	£	%
Clearing & other domestic banks	34.7	80.0	11.2	17.0	45.9	42.1
British overseas & commonwealth banks	3.3	7.4	11.1	16.9	14.4	13.2
American banks	4.1	9.2	24.7	37.4	28.8	26.4
Foreign banks & affiliates	1.0	2.3	9.4	14.2	10.4	9.2
Other overseas banks	0.5	1.1	9.7	14.5	10.2	9.1
Total	43.6	100.0	66.1	100.0	109.7	100.0

Source: Bank of England, *Quarterly Bulletin*.

The British Overseas & Commonwealth Banks represent long-standing London connections that in the past serviced the foreign trade financing and sterling liquidity requirements of peripheral members of the Commonwealth and Sterling Area. More recently these institutions have expanded their London activities to include Eurocurrency and corporate financing. Representation in this group is weighted heavily with Canadian, Australian, and Far Eastern institutions. A number of these institutions are referred to as 'Immigrant Banks' reflecting their growing interest in servicing individuals from their home countries who have taken up residence in London.

The American Banks include approximately fifty institutions which rank as the largest in the U.S. Nearly all of the American banks are relative newcomers, most having established London offices since 1965. The London *branches* of

American banks rank with the largest non-American banks in size, and conduct a wholesale, Eurocurrency operation. The American banks have been aggressively seeking to develop the sterling side of their deposit and lending business, and hold close to 9 per cent of U.K. sterling deposits. In addition, several American banks are represented in London by interests in consortium banks which specialise in intermediate term Eurocurrency loans. Finally, a few of the largest American banks have been moving in the direction of providing consumer financial services so as to establish a broader retail base of operations in the U.K.

The remaining categories of foreign banks include a diversity of Continental European, Far Eastern, Socialist-Comecon, Middle East, and Latin American institutions. Prominently included are German, Swiss, Japanese, French, Italian, Scandinavian, Chinese, Brazilian, and Malayan banking institutions. These banks provide access to London financing of foreign trade for home country business firms, carry out sterling money market activities for their parent institutions and customers, effect stock market transactions in London for head office, and funnel information concerning business opportunities and credit market conditions.

From the preceding discussion it should be clear that foreign banks have pre-empted a disproportionate share of the banking business in the U.K., as measured on the deposit side of the balance sheet. This has taken place without anxiety by the London banking community or the U.K. authorities. In fact, the U.K. authorities have fostered this development.

B. ADVANTAGES IN U.K. LOCATION

Foreign banks derive numerous advantages from direct London representation. Perhaps the most important asset is relative freedom from regulation. A second important feature of London is the large reservoir of technical expertise that exists there. A large part of the attraction of London as an international banking centre is the encouragement shown towards the development of the Eurocurrency market by the Bank of England. The flexibility of the Bank of England in encouraging growth of the Eurocurrency market is in sharp contrast to the legalistic and almost bureaucratic approach to banking supervision on the Continent and in the United States.

Finally, diversification and the mixed banking pattern have become part of the style of banking in the U.K. This has been fostered by competition among newcomer foreign banks, especially the American institutions.

While foreign banks have continued to find London an attractive base of operation, the British authorities have reacted even more positively to the prospects of furthering the development of London as an international financial entrepot. There are sound reasons for this policy. A major factor has been the desire to further enhance the status of domestic banks in the U.K., which derive considerable advantages from the contacts and referral business that accrues to indigenous banks operating from a base that increasingly assumes financial entrepot status. The rationalisation movement that has taken place among the large clearing banks in the late 1960s reflects the influence of international competitive pressures and the growing need to adapt to a changing environment. The prosperity enjoyed by the merchant banks in London further attests to the need to maintain London's status as a major international financial centre. Further, we should recognise that the competitive pressures generated in London by the liberal open policy of the British authorities towards foreign banking has compelled indigenous banking institutions to become more flexible and adaptive. The more flexible monetary policy in the U.K. of the past five years further indicates this officially supported move toward enhancing banking and financial market efficiency by means of stimulating competition. In turn, this has benefitted domestic banking institutions.

A second factor explaining the British policy of welcoming foreign banking institutions has been the combination of strong financial markets and a weak currency. The U.K. money and capital markets rank among the largest and most efficient in the world. Unfortunately, it has not been possible to open up these markets to non-resident borrowers due to the weakness of the British balance of payments. Consequently, the U.K. authorities have attempted to restore London's role by rebuilding the entrepot aspects of international banking and financing business. In this respect they have been most successful.

London functions as a wholesale centre for Eurodollar transactions, London institutions play a dominant role in most areas of the Eurocurrency market, specialised London-based consortium banks have been established to engage in intermediate term lending, London institutions play a major role and are well represented in Eurobond flotations, and the London money and capital markets have been strengthened as a result of the ancillary business derived from a growing financial entrepot business.

A third factor that has been important to the British authorities in attracting foreign banking institutions is the important role played by invisible earnings in the U.K. balance of payments. Private U.K. invisible earnings account for one-third of Britain's total foreign income. In the mid-1960s the United States and United Kingdom together accounted for over 41 per cent of world invisible earnings, with the U.K. total dominated by shipping and investment income receipts.[1] Other invisible earnings, including merchanting and banking receipts, are closely linked to the role of sterling as an international currency, the efficiency and competitiveness of the financial institutions in the United Kingdom, and the close links between British firms and their overseas customers. Invisible earnings play a highly important and strategic role in the U.K. balance of payments by offsetting persistent trade deficits.

While invisible earnings of U.K. banks account for a relatively small proportion of the total, they represent one of the most rapidly growing components. Moreover, we must look beyond bank invisible earnings to appreciate fully the contribution of foreign banks to London's financial market efficiency and to U.K. invisible earnings. Foreign banks bring a considerable amount of 'other business' to London including the placement of orders to buy and sell securities on the London Stock Exchange, the purchase and sale of money market assets, sterling acceptance and bill financing, sterling and Eurocurrency loans to resident borrowers, the handling of documents for foreign trade transactions and financing, and investment portfolio management. Much of the earnings of domestic U.K. banks is from foreign banks that have offices in London, and which are not classified as non-residents for balance of payments purposes. Hence, much of the U.K. banking sectors 'invisible earnings' are not reflected since they do not fit into balance of payments categories.

A final factor is the need to service the foreign investments of British residents overseas and of foreign investors in the United Kingdom. The U.K. ranks second behind the United States as a long-term direct investor and as a recipient of direct investment inflows from non-resident business firms. Similarly, Britain ranks second behind the U.S. in long-term portfolio (securities) investments. The presence of foreign banks facilitates foreign (inward) investment in the U.K., and thereby strengthens the balance of payments accounts. Moreover, the foreign exchange proceeds of such inward investments provides the international purchasing power to maintain and even extend British overseas investments, which have been an important contributor to U.K. invisible receipts. There is little doubt that the British feel that foreign business investment (assisted by the presence of foreign banks) has brought beneficial effects through increased competition, new technology, and improved managerial and organisational approaches.

C. COMPARISON OF U.K. AND U.S.

The United Kingdom and United States present interesting and valuable comparisons from the standpoint of their serving as host countries for foreign banking institutions. While the U.K. has a longer history as a host country for foreign banks, the United States has been narrowing the absolute gap, and in some respects may be considered to have gained on the U.K.

In this section we compare the U.K. and U.S. as international banking centres in four essential areas. These include (1) foreign banking structure, (2) role as an international deposit centre, (3) money market, and (4) capital market. The focus of our discussion is the relative importance and advantages of each country in each of these areas.

1. FOREIGN BANKING STRUCTURE

Foreign banking structure is reflected by the number of foreign banking offices of domestic banks, as well as by the number of foreign banks represented in the banking centre country. United Kingdom banks appear to have a substantial edge over American banks in both areas. We should note that many of the foreign banking offices of U.K. banks now operate as local or indigenous banks in the countries where they are located. This local banking flavour has tended to increase over time, and these banking offices may neither contribute to the international importance of London as a world banking centre nor carry out significant international banking operations. By comparison, the foreign branches of American banks tend to operate on a more transnational basis, and the largest branches holding the lion's share of resources are heavily dependent on Eurocurrency, multinational corporate, and wholesale transactions volume. The asset growth of American overseas branches has been considerable, and has even penetrated the U.K. sterling market. Recent endeavours of the large London clearing banks to develop a broader (including U.S.) base of overseas operations is a logical reaction to the increasing penetration of foreign banks in the U.K. deposit and loan markets, and can be viewed as a favourable (pro-competitive) development.

London has long functioned as the international banking centre of the world, and only recently has New York been able to challenge London's supremecy in this area. Foreign banks are attracted to London for a multitude of reasons. Longstanding financial and political relationships between the home country and the U.K. rank high among these factors. Equally important is the tolerant attitude of the British authorities; the minimum amount of formal regulation and supervision applied to banks in general and foreign banks in particular; the open and competitive Eurocurrency market which is centred in London; the vast assortment of internationally oriented financial and non-financial services headquartered in London including insurance, commodities, shipping and freight handling; and the orientation of British industry and business toward world affairs and overseas connections. New York and California have grown to challenge London in several of these areas. Nevertheless, numerous advantages continue to accrue on London's side.

2. ROLE AS INTERNATIONAL DEPOSIT CENTRE

The United Kingdom and United States jointly share leadership as international deposit centres. The U.S. plays a

Comparison of International Banking Role of United Kingdom and United States 1973

	Billions of currency units	
	United States $	United Kingdom £ / $[d]

	United States $	United Kingdom £	United Kingdom $[d]
Foreign Banking Structure:			
1. Foreign banking offices of domestic banks[a]	691	2,242	
2. Number of foreign banks represented in country	164	226	
Role as International Deposit Centre:			
3. Foreign deposits in local currency	18.4	2.46	5.90
4. Foreign currency deposits			
of residents	—	18.70	44.88
of non-residents	—	31.36	75.26
Money Market:			
5. Money market assets[b]	224.8	20.00	48.00
6. Short-term liabilities to foreigners	69.2	5.70	13.68
7. Short-term liabilities as percentage of money market assets	30.8%	28.7%	
8. Foreign loans and other claims of banks			
local currency	26.60	1.32	3.17
foreign currency	—	31.34	75.22
Capital Market:			
9. Foreign bond issues	1.37	159.9 mill	383.7 mill
10. Foreign ownership of domestic stocks and bonds	40.3[c]	5.00[c]	12.00[c]

[a] Refers to branches and agencies of parent bank. Excludes banking offices of affiliate banking institutions separately incorporated in host country.
[b] For U.S. includes Treasury bills, commercial paper, negotiable CDs, bankers' acceptances, federal funds, and loans to brokers. For U.K. includes discount market assets, sterling CDs, money at call from banks, bank holdings of short and medium-term government securities, sterling loans to local authorities and bankers' acceptances.
[c] Data refer to 1972.
[d] Converted to dollars at rate of $2.40 = £1.00.

Source: Board of Governors, *Federal Reserve Bulletin*; Bank of England, *Quarterly Bulletin*.

somewhat more important role than the U.K. for several reasons (Line 3, Table 8-2). First, the dollar has enjoyed greater stability of value than the pound sterling. Second, the dollar has functioned as an international loan and investment currency. Sterling has not been able to function as effectively in this respect due to balance of payments difficulties and the need to impose exchange restrictions on the granting of sterling credits to non-residents. Third, the dollar has played the role of an international transactions and vehicle currency, and this has tended to enhance its acceptability as a currency in which short-term investments might be held.

Despite the preceding, London plays a more important role than New York when we consider non-resident holdings of foreign and local currency deposits (Line 3 and 4, Table 8-2). Since money market assets can be held in lieu of bank deposits, it is appropriate also to consider the total of short-term liabilities to foreigners denominated in local currency. In this comparison New York functions as a larger international deposit centre.

3. MONEY MARKET

The money markets in the U.K. and U.S. are the largest in the world, and service a wide assortment of residents and non-residents who deposit funds or borrow on a short-term basis. In absolute terms the U.S. money market is several times larger than its counterpart in the United Kingdom (Line 5, Table 8-2). Nevertheless, the U.K. market is equally efficient, and enjoys a broad diversity of credit types including assets of the discount market, negotiable sterling CDs, money at call from banks, central government securities, loans to local authorities and bankers' acceptances. Both markets exhibit a high proportion of non-resident ownership of assets outstanding (28–30 per cent of total), and both reflect the international deposit and clearing functions performed by London and New York.

We should remember that the London market enjoys an important adjunct sector, namely the Eurodollar market which is centred in that city. The volume of foreign currency deposits in London banks by far exceeds the volume of money market assets outstanding in the U.K., and if we add these to U.K. money market assets the total comes close to the size of the U.S.

money market. In short, London based financial institutions derive considerable advantages from the existence of Eurodollar trading facilities, a technical advantage that could not be offset by the U.S. unless considerable incentives were afforded to New York institutions in the direction of trading in foreign currency funds.

Finally, we should note that U.S. banks have provided loans and other credits to non-residents (Line 8, Table 8-2) which far exceed those provided by U.K. institutions. However, if we include foreign currency loans U.K. based banks are several times as important as U.S. institutions.

4. CAPITAL MARKET

The traditional role of London as an exporter of capital has been well described. Unfortunately, economic vicissitudes and structural changes in world payments have impaired the ability of the United Kingdom to serve as a source of long-term investment capital for several decades. Nevertheless, foreign bond issues worth several hundred million dollars are sold in the London capital market each year. Some of these issues involve the refunding of existing indebtedness, and others represent issues of sterling area members that have enjoyed preferential access to the London capital market.

The U.S. capital markets far outdistance all others in size, diversity, and efficiency. In recent years foreign bond issues placed in the U.S. capital market have ranged between $1.2–$1.6 billion per annum. Removal of the Interest Equalization Tax early in 1974 should result in an expansion of foreign issues in New York, but it is not possible to project this trend clearly due to recent uncertainties and growing competition in the world financial markets.

While London may not be as attractive a centre for foreign banks as in earlier years due to the foreign exchange constraint imposed on the export of British capital, it continues to draw foreign banks interested in participating in secondary market (portfolio) trading on the London Stock Exchange. The London and New York Stock Exchanges both tend to attract foreign banks for purposes of facilitating securities transactions for the account of customers of their respective parent banks. The London and New York markets offer a broad diversity of securities for investment purposes, effect transactions at relatively low cost, and provide continuous and relatively stable trading market opportunities.

D. LESSON FROM THE UNITED KINGDOM

Similarities in economic structure and financial market development suggest that the United States could benefit from a careful analysis of British policy toward foreign banking activities. The Bank of England and government officials have long maintained an open door policy toward foreign banks wishing to establish London offices. The U.K. has derived considerable advantages from this policy, since foreign banks have made positive contributions to economic and financial market performance. These contributions have taken the form of facilitating the inflow of foreign investment, strengthening the balance of payments position, and permitting London to serve as a financial entrepot. In turn foreign investment flows have added to the invisible earnings of the British economy. The volume of international business handled by U.K. banks also has increased. Finally, competition in the U.K. financial markets has been enhanced.

Differences between the American and British banking systems raise the question 'Can we make the analogy concerning opening the door to foreign banks?' The major differences between the U.S. and British banking systems appear to centre on the preservation of regional sub-markets in the various states in the United States, the more inward-looking attitude of medium-size and small American banks, and the complete absence of international orientation characteristic among the smaller American institutions. Each of these differences could be important in arriving at a consensus concerning the applicability of an open door policy.

Regulatory agencies in the United States have long been guided by the McFadden Act which prohibits banking across state lines.[2] As noted in our discussion in Chapter 5 the artificial separation of banking and credit markets into fifty state jurisdictions has been breaking down. The growth orientation of large American banks and the multi-state activities of foreign banks have both been important factors in the trend toward unification of banking and credit markets. From the point of view of financial market efficiency considerable advantages could accrue to the United States from a closer integration of banking and credit markets across state lines. Therefore any increase in competition resulting from the entry of additional foreign banks into the United States would be welcome.

Smaller American banks have remained aloof as far as active competition in the larger national and international loan and deposit markets is concerned. This is unfortunate since a large part of locally generated deposit funds remains unavailable to compete in geographically wider loan markets. This contrasts with the U.K. situation where the clearing banks operate in all corners of the economy and where foreign banks tend to heighten the mobility of funds passing through London.

To summarise, differences between the U.S. and U.K. banking systems do not offer a basis for rejecting the analogy. In fact, the differences discussed above tend to reinforce the thesis that the United States should pursue an open door policy toward foreign banks, similar to that followed by the British.

The United Kingdom has pursued a highly rational and pragmatic policy vis-à-vis foreign banks. As a result London hosts a large number of foreign banking institutions from which the United Kingdom derives considerable advantages. Similar advantages might be expected to accrue to the United States should it maintain an open door policy toward foreign banks.

9 Problems and Issues

> America cannot be an ostrich
> with its head in the sand.
>
> Woodrow Wilson

In preceding chapters we viewed the rapid growth of foreign banking in the United States, and noted that the period 1965–75 has witnessed at least a partial internationalisation of the American banking system and credit markets. At yearend 1974 foreign banks in the U.S. held $56 billion in resources, representing over 6 per cent of the assets in the U.S. banking system. The following discussion focuses on three basic questions. Are the effects from this expansion of foreign banks in the U.S. on balance beneficial or harmful? What problems have been created as a result of the expansion of foreign banking in the United States? And do the regulatory proposals of 1973–75 (discussed in Chapter 7) effectively deal with the real issues posed by the growth of foreign banking in the U.S.?

The influx of foreign banks to the United States over the past decade has probably generated more beneficial than harmful effects. On the positive side competition has been stimulated in the bank credit markets, the presence of foreign banks has attracted inflows of capital funds, the financial entrepot role of the U.S. has been magnified, and the banking system has been strengthened. These benefits must be compared with much less important negative effects that include somewhat greater difficulties in enforcing monetary policy measures, and the existence of unfair competitive advantages for foreign as compared with domestic banks. U.S. monetary policy is not unduly hampered by the presence of foreign banks in the U.S., since only marginal changes in credit market liquidity can be effected by foreign bank lending activity in the U.S. credit markets. Moreover, we have seen that the unfair competitive advantages of foreign banks tend to be exaggerated. Therefore, it is this writer's opinion that thus far the beneficial effects which follow from the growing presence of foreign banks in the United States far outweigh any possible negative effects.

Increased competition from foreign banks has tended to destroy monopoly influences in local banking markets, and has created a new environment of change in the U.S. banking structure. In specific cases foreign banks have strengthened the U.S. banking system by absorbing weak banks. Often this has taken place in situations or under conditions that would not permit large domestic banks to acquire the weak bank. In 1974 Lloyds Bank Ltd. acquired the First Western Bank & Trust Company, a domestic institution that had suffered from weak management. In the same year the European American Bank & Trust acquired the assets of the Franklin National Bank, an institution that had gone through dilution of capital funds as a result of faulty banking practices. Early in 1974 when the Franklin National Bank difficulties became publicised, that institution ranked twentieth in size among major banking institutions in the U.S. In 1975 the Bank of Tokyo of California submitted a plan to acquire a large California bank that had experienced management difficulties. In each of these cases acquisition of the U.S. bank by another large domestic banking institution would have proven difficult due to the fear of bank monopoly, and the inability to resort to out-of-state domestic banks for such acquisitions. In this connection in 1975 a legislative proposal was submitted to the U.S. Congress that would permit bank holding companies to absorb weak banks in another state.

A review of the regulatory proposals submitted to Congress in the period 1973–75 raises several questions. First, is an elaborate system of federal chartering and supervision of foreign banks really necessary? Second, would the creation of federal supervisory powers over foreign banks deal with the real issues and problems? Third, will Congress work toward strengthening the U.S. financial markets so that they may play a more important role in world finance, and will that strengthening be coordinated with the mechanism for regulating and supervising foreign banks in the U.S.?

In Chapter 7 we reviewed the reasons underlying the legislative proposals vis-à-vis foreign banking institutions. The major reasons offered were to strengthen monetary policy and control capital flows, to assure reciprocity, to place domestic banks on a par with foreign banks, and to prevent undesirable changes in banking structure. These reasons were found to be incomplete or lacking in substance. Foreign banks represent a minor escape valve insofar as domestic monetary policy is concerned. Moreover, the international divisions of large American banks represent a potentially greater escape valve insofar as monetary policy measures are concerned. To raise the question of reciprocity implies that American banks have not been able to effectively negotiate with foreign governments for direct access to their banking markets. On the contrary, American banks are well represented overseas and it is difficult to make the case that they require more effective reciprocity relationships. The contention that foreign banks enjoy unfair advantages over domestic banks must be evaluated in broad perspective. Any nonmember domestic bank enjoys the same 'advantages' as foreign banks insofar as U.S. reserve requirements are concerned. Advantages of foreign banks relating to ownership of domestic securities affiliates tend to be overemphasised. Foreign banks are not important factors in the securities markets, and American banks provide collateral services in these areas. Advantages relating to interstate operations of foreign banks should be examined in light of the artificial separation of American banking markets into fifty state systems. We have seen that the extent of interstate operations of foreign banks is no greater than in the case of domestic banks which operate across state lines via holding companies, Edge Act affiliates, and nonbank affiliates.

The grounds offered in support of extending federal regulation over foreign banks are weak. It is doubtful that the American banking system will benefit to any great extent as a result of this type of extension of federal chartering and supervisory authority.

No doubt the appearance of serious problems in international banking in 1974 accentuated the interest in the United States in safeguarding the integrity of deposit banking. These problems included the Franklin National Bank debacle, wherein the Federal Reserve Bank of New York extended loans to that distressed institution of $1.7 billion. A major cause of

Franklin National's difficulty was its foreign exchange operations. Like many other banks Franklin had expanded its international banking activities at a rapid pace. As a result of the Franklin National episode there developed deep concern regarding the foreign exchange activities of all commercial banks, and especially of those foreign banks in the U.S. whose head offices operate chiefly in foreign currencies.

The Bankhaus Herstatt failure provided additional cause for concern. Up to the time of the Herstatt failure the German banking system had been regarded as inviolable. This failure reduced confidence in the international payments mechanism and raised fears of bankrupt institutions dragging down solvent banks. The effects rippled into the Eurocurrency market where a tiered interest rate pattern appeared as quality became the watchword.

The preceding events focused interest on the potential pitfalls of international banking, and provided support for extending federal regulatory powers over foreign banks in the United States. However, these events had no direct bearing on the fundamental issues at stake. The real issues in the expansion of foreign banking in the United States relate to the following:

1. Should foreign banks be free to introduce competition in the financial markets at the expense of local, entrenched, monopoly banks. The American banking system is broken up into fifty separate state systems, and as a result there are numerous local monopoly market situations.
2. Should innovative American banks continue to be circumscribed by archaic prohibitions on branching (interstate and intrastate)? Hopefully, New York and California will act speedily to enact reciprocal branching legislation as a first step in relaxing restrictions against interstate branching. Until that takes place, it will be possible to argue that foreign banks with interstate operations enjoy unfair advantage over American banks.
3. Should statutory restrictions that attempt to separate deposit from investment banking be maintained, even if they deprive segments of the securities industry from

additional venture capital and offshore business volume? Moreover, should American banks be prevented from operating in the investment banking area, even though they already have found indirect means of providing investment banking services? American banks participate in the new issues business overseas, and could possibly increase their participation in this activity in the U.S. indirectly via their offshore affiliates. The large U.S. commercial banks represent a major future potential source of capital infusion, know-how, and financial technology for this lagging sector of the American financial markets.
4. Is a healthy and prosperous foreign banking community needed to strengthen the U.S. as an international financial intermediary, especially in the case of intermediating petrodollar funds? Here we have noted that foreign banks can play an important role in attracting and investing petrodollars, and enhance the desirability of using New York as a financial entrepot for these international flows of funds.

To summarise, the real issues regarding entry and expansion of foreign banks in the United States appear to focus on problems inherent in the present structure and supervision of the American banking system. Unlike other countries the U.S. does not periodically review and analyse its banking system to determine needs and priorities. The Canadian banking system is reviewed every decade and legislative proposals are an ultimate product of this review. The American banking system is reviewed only after crisis, and any legislative proposals that follow tend to be in the form of an over-reaction. The Hunt Commission Report published in 1971 provided a basis for implementing financial market reforms in the U.S., but largely ignored the question of international banking relationships. This was unfortunate.

A careful study of the role and importance of foreign banking in the U.S. should precede any legislative action conferring supervisory authority on federal banking agencies. That study should be integrated with an analysis of the possible need for reform of financial institutions in the U.S. so that a coordinated approach can be realised. In this way the U.S. financial markets may be further strengthened in a manner that will permit the most effective use of foreign banks as an integral part of the financial framework.

Appendix A

Statement of Condition of Foreign Bank Branches, Agencies, Investment Companies, and Subsidiary Banks in the U.S., 31 December 1974

Millions of dollars

Account	All Institutions	Agencies, Branches and New York Investment Companies	Subsidiary Commercial Banks
ASSETS			
1. Cash and due from other banks	8,091	5,432	2,659
2. Bonds, stocks and other securities	3,908	1,618	2,290
U.S. Treasury securities	1,042	503	539
3. Loans	28,964	22,842	6,122
To commercial banks in U.S.	3,446	3,093	353
To banks in foreign countries	2,459	2,399	60
Commercial and industrial loans	19,210	16,132	3,077
To parties in U.S.	14,960	12,107	2,852
To parties in foreign countries	4,250	4,025	225
4. Customers' liabilities on acceptances outstanding	2,505	2,305	200
5. Customers' liabilities on deferred payment letters of credit	152	138	14
6. Due from directly related institutions	11,237	11,163	75
7. Other assets	1,310	808	502
8. Total Assets	56,167	44,305	11,862

Millions of dollars

Account	All Institutions	Agencies, Branches and New York Investment Companies	Subsidiary Commercial Banks
LIABILITIES			
9. Demand deposits or credit balances due from other than directly related institutions	9,794	5,207	4,587
10. Time and savings deposits	8,878	4,313	4,565
Time deposits due to IPC in foreign countries	1,448	1,267	181
Time deposits due to foreign governments and central banks	1,230	1,082	148
Time deposits due to commercial banks in foreign countries	1,201	967	244
11. Borrowing from other institutions	12,759	12,352	407
12. Liabilities on acceptances outstanding	2,415	2,210	204
13. Liabilities on deferred payment letters of credit	199	185	14
14. Other liabilities to other than directly related institutions	1,243	867	376
15. Due to directly related institutions	19,327	18,648	680
16. Reserves for bad debt losses and other reserves	270	194	77
17. Reserves for contingencies	85	76	9
18. Capital accounts	1,553	524	1,029
19. Total liabilities, reserves and capital accounts	56,167	44,305	11,862
Total claims on foreigners	15,682	15,023	659
Total liabilities to foreigners	22,634	20,290	2,344
Net foreign position	−6,952	−5,267	−1,685
Number of institutions reporting	158	130	28

Source: Board of Governors of the Federal Reserve System.

Appendix B

Summary of New York Superintendent's Denial of Barclays Acquisition of Long Island Trust Company

On 9 May 1973 the New York State Superintendent of Banks transmitted to the State Banking Board his recommendation to disapprove the application of Barclays Bank Ltd. and Barclays Bank International Ltd. to acquire the stock of Long Island Trust Company. According to the Superintendent this was the first time that the New York State Banking Board, or any banking authority in the United States, had considered an application by a major foreign bank to acquire a substantial interest in a domestic bank.

Background
At yearend 1972 the Long Island Trust Company of Garden City, Long Island, had total assets of $508 million and operated 32 offices. While LIT was the second largest bank headquartered in Nassau-Suffolk, its deposits and offices were exceeded by a number of other banks operating in that region. The Security National Bank was the largest Nassau-Suffolk headquarters bank, possessing four times the assets and two-and-a-half times the number of banking offices of LIT. LIT's business is retail oriented, and the bank has not actively sought to expand in the direction of offering full service banking to large corporate customers as have many of its larger competitors on Long Island. In 1972 LIT had approximately 7.3% of local deposits and 6.3% of banking offices.

The Barclays Group consists of Barclays Bank Limited and Barclays Bank International Limited, and their subsidiaries and affiliates around the globe. In 1972 the group held worldwide assets of $24 billion. Barclays Bank Limited is a U.K. bank, and a 'foreign bank holding company' registered with the Federal Reserve Board under the Bank Holding Company Act.

BBL is one of the leading British commercial banks and is actively engaged in retail banking in the U.K. Barclays Bank International Limited is a wholly-owned subsidiary of BBL, with assets of $9 billion, and 1,663 banking offices outside the U.K. In 1972 Barclays total U.S. assets amounted to $430 million, including $140 million in assets in Barclays Bank of California. In New York State Barclays maintained one branch office in New York City, a convenience office at JFK airport, and Barclays Bank of New York which had a Westchester branch. The total assets of BBIL in New York State amounted to about $289 million.

The Superintendent's Denial

In his review of the case the New York Superintendent noted that several issues had to be considered in arriving at a decision. These included the question of reciprocity, and the question of antitrust and competitive effects.

In examining the meaning and intent of reciprocity the Superintendent held that reciprocity does not mean 'that a foreign banking organization should be permitted to acquire a local bank where a New York City based holding company of comparable size would be denied the same acquisition'. According to the Superintendent's line of reasoning, to do otherwise would result in an unfair double standard tending to favour foreign banks. A large part of the Superintendent's discussion concerning reciprocity examines the different nature of American banking in the United Kingdom, i.e. the wholesale, de novo, merchant banking orientation.

The New York Superintendent viewed the lessening of potential competition between Barclays and LIT in the Nassau-Suffolk market as a reason for denying the proposed acquisition. Three points support the argument. First, the affected banking market is subject to rather high concentration with four banks holding about 50% of banking offices. Second, Barclays has the capability to enter the Nassau-Suffolk area through a smaller acquisition. Finally, approval of this application could lead to substantial new acquisitions by large New York banking organisations in other markets around the State.

Comments on Denial

The Superintendent's thesis is persuasive. First, it is suggested that concentration in the immediate banking market is high, and that LIT is the second largest independent bank in the State. Examination of the concentration of banking offices of the ten largest banking groups in Nassau-Suffolk indicates the following. LIT ranks fourth in number of offices, but probably should be ranked somewhat lower in overall competitive ability. Five New York City based holding company groups operate between 23 and 25 banking offices in Nassau-Suffolk. Moreover, these holding company groups are backed up by the rather substantial resources of their parent organisations, far beyond the scope of LIT. Moreover, the first three ranking banks by number of offices (Franklin National, Security, and National Bank of North America) were several times larger than LIT and operated a diversified banking business including corporate as well as retail operations.

Second, it is suggested that the Barclays Group has the financial capability to enter Nassau-Suffolk through a smaller acquisition. The question that emerges at this point is 'how much smaller' and 'for what reason?' LIT operates 6.3% of the banking offices in the area. Would acquisition of a bank with 1% of the banking offices produce an increase in competition in the area? It might take a decade for Barclays to build a small acquired bank into a significant competitive factor in the market area. However, an increase in the competitive situation could result from Barclays acquiring a bank that is of sufficient size to become an important factor given the support and assistance of a large bank such as Barclays.

In 1973 LIT faced competition from three substantial Nassau-Suffolk banks which were considerably larger than LIT itself. Moreover, five substantial New York City holding company groups were well represented in the Nassau-Suffolk market area. These New York City institutions each provided many billions of dollars of backup to their Nassau-Suffolk operations. Moreover, they complemented their Nassau-Suffolk affiliates very adequately by their specialisation in the corporate services departments. In the words of the Superintendent:

> the locally available resources of the major New York

holding companies, together with their numerous local offices, long-standing customer relationships, customer identification and goodwill, knowledge of the market and retail banking experience in local markets give them a significant edge over a foreign banking organization such as Barclays in the competition for retail banking business, including savings deposits, checking accounts and consumer credit.[1]

Strengthening LIT by permitting it to become part of the Barclays Group could have led to a greater degree of workable competition in the Nassau-Suffolk banking market.

The New York decision denying Barclays the right to acquire LIT carried with it serious implications for the future development of banking ties between the United States and the rest of the world. The Barclays–LIT decision placed U.S. regulatory agencies in a paradoxical situation. American and foreign bankers were watching for possible clues of U.S. policy concerning domestic bank acquisitions by overseas banking organisations. Rejection of another foreign bank request to acquire a large domestic bank would reinforce foreign suspicions that the U.S. was following a protectionist policy in the banking field. On the other hand, approval of a takeover of a major U.S. bank by a foreign bank at the State regulatory level might trigger Federal control of foreign bank operations in the United States.

Crucial to the whole question of foreign bank acquisitions of domestic banks is that of ultimate regulatory authority. Who should regulate foreign banking in the United States? It is not surprising that shortly after the Barclays denial several foreign banking control bills were submitted in the U.S. Congress.

Notes

CHAPTER 3
1. *American Banker*, 'Sanwa Bank to Issue Large CDs in U.S.' 23 June 1975, p. 14.
2. In April 1975 it was announced that the Bank of Tokyo of California was negotiating to purchase the Southern California First National Bank, which held deposits of $770 million at that time.
3. In 1975 Stafford R. Grady, Chairman of the Board of the $1 billion deposit Lloyds Bank, California was elected president of the California Bankers Association. This is the first time that the California Bankers Association has been headed by an officer of a California subsidiary of a foreign bank.

CHAPTER 4
1. As a bank holding company, these foreign banks become subject to the supervisory authority of the Board of Governors of the Federal Reserve System.
2. Remarks attributed to William T. Dwyer, Vice President, First National Bank of Chicago, in the *American Banker*, 29 November 1973. According to Mr. Dwyer, the ten largest commercial banks and bank holding companies in the U.S. are planning to establish 5,700 domestic offices across the United States.

CHAPTER 5
1. Peter Brunsden, 'Building a U.S. Branch Network', *The Banker*, January 1974, p. 41.
2. P. F. Roden, L. J. James, G. A. Saussy, and D. A. Nettleton, *Louisiana's Debate Over Multibank Holding Companies* (Division of Business and Economic Research, University of New Orleans, 1974) p. 19.
3. This was the largest foreign owned banking institution in the U.S. until Lloyds Bank Ltd. acquired the First Western Bank & Trust Co., Los Angeles in 1973. In 1974 the European American Bank & Trust Co. acquired the Franklin National Bank, the resulting institution becoming the largest foreign owned bank in the U.S.
4. It is not necessary for a foreign bank to possess direct U.S. representation to participate in loans to U.S. companies or other U.S. borrowers. It is simply necessary that the foreign bank hold sizeable dollar balances or have ready access to such balances. The Eurodollar market provides this access. See Geoffrey Bell, *The Euro-Dollar Market and the International Financial System* (Macmillan, 1973) pp. 103–4.
5. Fred H. Klopstock, 'Foreign Banks in the United States: Scope and

Growth of Operations', *Monthly Review* of the Federal Reserve Bank of New York, June 1973, p. 143.
6. These include the mandatory controls on U.S. direct investment initiated in 1968, the Interest Equalization Tax of 1964, and the voluntary foreign credit restraint administered by the Federal Reserve on bank lending abroad which began in 1965. See Francis A. Lees, *International Banking and Finance* (Macmillan/Halsted, 1974) pp. 255–6.
7. Lees, pp. 50–3.
8. This is done by assuming that the bulk of deposits in the largest banks is subject to international competition, and that deposits in all other banks are not subject to this competition. This assumption is an oversimplification but should provide workable comparisons.
9. This criterion is analogous to that used by the Federal Reserve Board in its 1974–75 proposals to regulate foreign banks. Under these proposals foreign banking institutions with worldwide assets of $500 million or more and direct representation in the U.S. would become subject to Federal Reserve jurisdiction as bank holding companies.
10. If we exclude multi-state representation via representative offices, 41 of these 53 foreign banks enjoyed interstate operations in 1974.
11. For example, in Texas the Constitutional Convention held in 1974 voted to reinsert a strengthened version of an existing prohibition against foreign corporations operating banks.
12. Geoff. Brouillette, 'California Bars Half of Recent Foreign Applicants', *American Banker*, 28 May 1974.
13. These include the Tokai Bank of California; the Japan-California Bank; the Korea Exchange Bank of California; the Bank of Nova Scotia of California; and the American-Asian Bank.
14. In the relatively short period December 1973–July 1974 short-term claims on foreigners reported by banks in the U.S. increased from $20.7 billion to $33.4 billion, or by 6 per cent.
15. S. I. Davis maintains that it is possible in future for the U.S. prime rate to adjust more flexibly with London Eurodollar rates, thereby narrowing the differential and providing increased opportunities for London based lending operations to compete more effectively with New York. 'Euro-loan Pricing: Back to the Drawing Board', *The Banker*, June 1974, pp. 558–9.
16. It is possible to argue that agencies funnel deposits to head offices outside the U.S., which in turn invest these funds in the New York money market or loan market via their agencies. In this way no FDIC assessments or reserve requirements apply.
17. At the time it was held that large U.S. banks could pull reserves away from smaller banks that did not possess foreign branch offices with direct access to Eurodollar deposits.

CHAPTER 6
1. A disadvantage in this respect is that in cases of investments where synergy is available it is less likely that diversification can be enhanced.

NOTES

2. In the limiting case, when the correlation of returns on the two investments is negative one, the risk or standard deviation of the portfolio is entirely eliminated.
3. This analysis is further developed in a book the author recently completed titled *International Financial Markets* (Praeger Publishers: New York, 1975). The analysis is contained in Chapter 3 of this book.
4. Robert Leftwich, 'Foreign Direct Investments in the United States, 1962–71', *Survey of Current Business*, February 1973, pp. 32–3.
5. Leftwich, p. 33.
6. In 1973 the gross purchases and sales of U.S. equities by foreign investors was $12.7 billion and $9.9 billion, respectively.
7. We should further note that a NYSE public transaction study indicates that in the short period 1969–71 foreign transactions on the Big Board (NYSE) increased in relative importance from 2.3 per cent to 5.2 per cent of total trading.
8. James H. Lorie, *Public Policy for American Capital Markets* (U.S. Treasury Department, 1974) pp. 18–19.
9. Exceptions include Canadian firms which are permitted NYSE membership. The American Stock Exchange has a similar prohibition but foreign securities firms are admitted to the regional exchanges.
10. It is feasible for American banks to 'match' customer trades in listed securities, without use of the services of stock exchange member firms. It has been reported to this writer that the volume of such trades has increased sharply in recent years, although there is no data covering such transactions.
11. In the period 1969–73 the number of NYSE member firms declined from 622 to 523. The largest single year change took place in 1969 when the number of member firms was reduced by 50.
12. In the period 1968–73 the price of a seat or membership on the NYSE declined precipitously from a high of $515,000 in 1968 to a low of $72,000 in 1973.
13. They might not have to acquire foreign funds directly. A main function of these foreign banks would be offshore lending from the U.S., which would accomplish a foreign exchange transfer of funds from the United States.

CHAPTER 7

1. Francis A. Lees, 'Foreign Investment in U.S. Banks', *Mergers & Acquisitions*, Fall 1973, p. 6.
2. An exception would be the legislation passed in 1960 permitting foreign banks to establish branch offices in New York.
3. This requirement is analogous to the capital-to-deposit ratio used in commercial banking as one of the measures of capital adequacy.
4. This is often referred to as the 'separate entity' concept and became an important practical issue in the case of failure of the Intra Bank, when the New York Superintendent made use of the assets of the New York branch of Intra to settle claims against that branch.
5. However, a customer may enter into an agreement (with an agency or investment company) to place a credit balance on a time basis having a

definite maturity. In such cases payment of interest may be permitted.
6. In the failure of the Intra Bank in 1966, several large U.S. banks claimed the right of setoff, intending to use deposit funds of the New York branch of Intra placed with them as an offset to general claims they held against the parent institution. As a result the New York Superintendent has directed that before such deposit funds can be considered eligible assets the depository bank must agree to waive all rights of setoff.
7. This was followed by Federal Reserve Board approval in December 1973.
8. California Superintendent of Banks, *Report on Foreign Banking Matters*, April 1974, p. 35.
9. *American Banker*, 'Bank of Tokyo, California, SCFNB Discuss Merger', 25 April 1975, pp. 3 & 30.
10. This clause was applied in 1975 when two Brazilian banks made application to establish branches in Chicago. The Illinois statute states that the commissioner's office must receive copies of the banking laws of a foreign nation relating to foreign branches in order for the Illinois regulator to approve the reciprocal establishment of branches in Chicago. In Brazil foreign banks are allowed to branch by presidential edict. *American Banker*, 'Illinois Bars Two Foreign Branches On Reciprocity Issue', 8 July 1975, pp. 1 & 11.
11. *Federal Reserve Bulletin*, October 1972, pp. 940–1.
12. It is even possible to argue that American banks enjoy advantages over foreign banks. In 1975 a California-based bank controlled by a Japanese parent institution was denied permission to establish a Texas-based Edge Act affiliate. Robert Dowling, 'Bank of Tokyo Plan For Houston Unit Rejected by Fed', *American Banker*, 3 June 1975.
13. Interestingly, this provision would have prohibited the acquisition of the Franklin National Bank by the European American Bank and Trust Company, and might have necessitated merger of Franklin National into a very large American bank.
14. An exception would be made in the case of New York State Investment Companies and joint ventures of foreign banks.
15. This was the application of Barclays Bank Ltd., London to acquire the Long Island Trust Company, Garden City, N.Y. A summary of the Superintendent's denial is included in Appendix B.

CHAPTER 8
1. William M. Clarke (ed.), *Britain's Invisible Earnings*, Report of the Committee on Invisible Exports, 1967, p. 26.
2. Stated more correctly, the McFadden Act brings commercial banks in the U.S. subject to federal supervision into conformity with state restrictions on interstate branching.

APPENDIX B
1. New York State Banking Department, 'Press Release—State Banking Board Disapproves Barclays Proposed Acquisition of Long Island Trust Company', 10 May 1973, pp. 18–19.

Selected References

Books & Monographs

Geoffrey Bell, *The Euro-Dollar Market and the International Financial System* (London: Macmillan, 1973).

John D. Daniels, *Recent Foreign Direct Manufacturing Investment in the United States* (New York: Praeger, 1971).

Nicholas Faith, *The Infiltrators* (New York: E. P. Dutton, 1972).

Francis A. Lees, *International Banking and Finance* (London: Macmillan, 1974; New York: Halsted, 1974).

Francis A. Lees and Maximo Eng, *International Financial Markets* (New York: Praeger, 1975).

Raymond F. Mikesell and H. Herbert Furth, *Foreign Dollar Balances and the International Role of the Dollar* (National Bureau of Economic Research, 1974).

P. F. Roden, L. J. James, G. A. Saussy and D. A. Nettleton, *Louisiana's Debate Over Multibank Holding Companies* (Division of Business & Economic Research, University of New Orleans, 1974).

Task Force on Promoting Increased Foreign Investment in U.S. Corporate Securities, *Report to the President* (U.S. Government Printing Office, 1964).

Articles

Caryl Austrian, 'New York Clearing House Members Unanimously Oppose New Federal Laws on Foreign Banks', *American Banker*, 26 March 1974.

M. E. Barrett and J. A. Gehrke, 'Significant Differences Between Japanese and American Business', *MSU Business Topics*, Winter 1974.

Robert A. Bennett, 'Edge Subsidiaries Spread Across Nation Seen as Further Step to Interstate Banking', *American Banker*, 17 April 1972.

Andrew F. Brimmer, 'Foreign Banking Institutions in the United States Money Market', *The Review of Economics and*

Statistics, February 1962.

Andrew F. Brimmer and Frederick R. Dahl, 'Growth of American International Banking: Implications for Public Policy', *Journal of Finance*, May 1975.

Peter Brunsden, 'Building a U.S. Branch Network', *The Banker*, January 1974.

Colin Clout, 'Foreign Banks in California', *The Banker*, March 1971.

The Conference Board, 'Announcements of Foreign Investments in U.S. Manufacturing Industries', *Press Release*, dated First Quarter 1974.

S. I. Davis, 'Euro-Loan Pricing: Back to the Drawing Board', *The Banker*, June 1974.

Richard A. Debs, 'International Banking', *Monthly Review* of the Federal Reserve Bank of New York, June 1975.

Robert Dowling, 'Bank of Tokyo Plan For Houston Unit Rejected by Fed', *American Banker*, 3 June 1975.

Franklin R. Edwards, 'Regulation of Foreign Banking in the United States: International Reciprocity and Federal-State Conflicts', *Columbia Journal of Transnational Law*, Winter 1974.

Edward P. Foldessy, 'Obscure Swiss Bank Allegedly Played Key Role in Franklin Banks Dealings', *Wall Street Journal*, 5 July 1974.

Cadogan A. Gordon, 'British Banking in New York', *The Banker*, July 1969.

Joseph D. Hutnyan, 'SEC Invites Comments on Propriety of Banks Entering Securities Field', *American Banker*, 1 May 1974.

Fred H. Klopstock, 'Foreign Banks in the United States: Scope and Growth of Operations', *Monthly Review* of the Federal Reserve Bank of New York, June 1973.

Francis A. Lees, 'Foreign Investment in U.S. Banks', *Mergers & Acquisitions*, Fall 1973.

Francis A. Lees, 'Which Route for Foreign Bank Regulation?', *Bankers Magazine*, Autumn 1974.

John E. Leimone, 'Edge Act Corporations: An Added Dimension to Southeastern International Banking', *Monthly Review*, Federal Reserve Bank of Atlanta, September 1974.

Sasumu Onoda, 'The Bank of Tokyo of California', *The Banker*, March 1971.

SELECTED REFERENCES

Frances W. Quantius, 'Elimination of Regulatory Inequities: Domestic vs. Foreign-Based U.S. Banks', *Bulletin of Business Research*, Ohio State University, September 1974.

Sanford Rose, 'What Really Went Wrong at Franklin National?', *Fortune*, October 1974.

James Rubenstein, 'FNB Chicago Maps National Expansion, Takes Steps for Interstate Branching', *American Banker*, 10 April 1974.

Charles N. Stabler, 'The Big Boards Foreign Problem', *Wall Street Journal*, 18 March 1974.

J. R. M. Van den Brink, 'Europe's Banks See Restrictions in U.S. as Regressive Measure', speech given at International Monetary Conference in Williamsburg, Virginia, reprinted in *American Banker*, 10 June 1974.

Richard S. Vokey, 'Foreign Banks in London', *The Banker*, October 1969.

C. Frederic Wiegold, 'Wriston Urges Nationwide Banking: Call Foreign Operations in U.S. Step in Right Direction', *American Banker*, 6 June 1974.

Jack Zwick, 'The Regulation of Foreign Banks in the United States', *National Banking Review*, September 1966.

Official Publications and Other Sources

Bank of England, *Quarterly Bulletin*, 1972–75.

Board of Governors of the Federal Reserve System, *Annual Reports*, 1971–74.

Board of Governors of the Federal Reserve System, *Federal Reserve Bulletin*, 1972–75.

Board of Governors of the Federal Reserve System, *Draft Outline*, Legislation on regulation of foreign bank activities in the United States, no date, 3 pages.

Jeffrey M. Bucher, 'Creative Tension in Banking', remarks at the Annual Convention of the Utah Bankers Association, St. George, Utah, 24 May 1974.

Arthur F. Burns, 'Letter to Hon. Wright Patman with Comments on H. R. 11440—The Foreign Bank Control Act', 16 February 1974.

California Superintendent of Banks, *Annual Reports*, 1970–74.

California Superintendent of Banks, *Report on Foreign Banking Matters*, April 1974.

SELECTED REFERENCES

Robert F. Cassidy, 'The Friendly Invasion: Foreign Banks in New York', unpublished dissertation, 1969.

Federal Deposit Insurance Corp., *Annual Reports*, 1971–73.

Federal Reserve Bank of Kansas City, 'Reserve Requirements: Part I, Comparative Reserve Requirements at Member and Nonmember Banks', *Monthly Review*, April 1974.

International Monetary Fund, *Annual Reports*, 1971–74.

International Monetary Fund, *International Financial Statistics*, 1972–75.

Joint Economic Committee, U.S. Congress, *Foreign Banking in the United States*, U.S. Government Printing Office, 1966. Also known as the Zwick Report.

Robert B. Leftwich, 'Foreign Direct Investments in the United States', *Survey of Current Business* (U.S. Department of Commerce, February 1973).

James H. Lorie, *Public Policy for American Capital Markets* (U.S. Treasury Department, 1974).

George W. Mitchell, Statement Before the Subcommittee on International Finance of the Committee on Banking, Housing and Urban Affairs, U.S. Senate, 23 January 1974.

George W. Mitchell, 'Multinational Banking in the United States: Some Regulatory Issues', remarks at the annual convention of the Bankers Association for Foreign Trade, Coronado, California, 8 April 1974.

George W. Mitchell, 'U.S. Regulatory and Monetary Policies and the International Operations of U.S. Banks', remarks at a conference on 'New York as a World Financial Center', New York City, 10 June 1974.

New York Superintendent of Banks, *Annual Reports*, 1970–74.

New York Superintendent of Banks, *Report of the Superintendent's Advisory Committee on Financial Reform*, March 1974.

Wright Patman, H. R. 11440, bill submitted to Committee on Banking and Currency, House of Representatives, 13 November 1973.

Thomas M. Rees, H. R. 11597, bill submitted to Committee on Banking and Currency, House of Representatives, 27 November 1973.

Index

ABD Securities Corp., 37
ABECOR Group, 37
ABN Corp., 37
acceptance credits, 27
acceptances, 9, 24, 61, 79, 98
acquisitions, 3
advantages, 17–18
 cost advantage, 64–5, 107
 of foreign banks, 64–6, 107–8, 111, 115, 120, 122, 123, 138, 140
 of New York, 63
 of U.S. banks, 154
agencies, 9, 17
 activities, 26, 34
 California, 29, 32
 capital required, 97
 during wartime, 12
 expansion phase, 12
 funnel funds, 152
 lending limits, 34
 liability management, 28
 licensing, 10, 11, 95
 New York, 26–7
 number of, 11, 12, 14
 source of funds, 27
 states authorising, 14
Algemene Bank Nederland, N.V., 37
Alien Property Custodian, 12
American Asian Bank, 152
American Bank of Lakeland, 102
American Investment Trust, N.V., 80
American Stock Exchange, 153
antitrust, 148
arbitrage, 64
 activities, 27
 funds, 20, 66–9
 opportunities, 70
armoured car services, 49
asset requirements, 99

BanCal Tri State Corp., 101

Banco di Roma, 37, 104
bank failures, 90
bank holding company, 33, 42, 45, 80, 151
 acquisitions, 36, 40, 103, 110, 123, 139
 act, 33, 36
 amendment of 1970, 103, 121
 avoidance, 120
 Barclays, 147
 dynamics, 47
 expansion, 18, 102
 Fed proposal, 114
 FRB jurisdiction, 102
 interstate, 46, 48, 49
 jurisdiction, 108, 116, 119
 number, 47
 state rules, 47
Bank Merger Act, 103
Bank of California, 101
Bank of England, 88, 128, 136
Bank of Japan, 27
Bank of Montreal, 11, 38
Bank of Nova Scotia of Calif., 152
Bank of Tokyo Ltd, 26, 30, 49
Bank of Tokyo of Calif., 50, 101, 139, 151
Bank of Tokyo Trust, New York, 26, 49
Banque de Bruxelles, 37
bankers acceptances, 27, 28, 49, 62, 98
Bankhaus I. D. Herstatt, 91, 141
Banking Act of 1933, 84, 119
banking laws, New York, 96–100
banking systems, 104, 118, 142
Barclays Bank of Calif., 30, 38, 49, 101, 148
Barclays Bank DCO, 11
Barclays Bank International, 38, 49, 147
Barclays Bank Ltd, 38, 49, 107, 147, 154
Barclays Bank of New York, 38, 49, 147
Basle Securities Corp., 37
Bayerische Hypotheken und Wechselbank, 37
bill of exchange, 11, 28, 30, 98

INDEX

Board of Governors, 36, 39, 49
bond issues, 4, 5
branching
  activities, 28, 35
  advantages, 35
  capital required, 97
  countywide, 48
  de novo, 18
  foreign bank interest, 48
  interstate, 109, 117, 141
  intrastate, 117, 118, 141
  licensing, 10, 95
  moratorium, 56–7
  New York enabling legislation, 28
  number, 14
  overseas, 3, 4
  prohibition, 46, 48
  reciprocal, 109, 113, 118, 125, 141
  restrictions, 18
  rules, 45
  state laws, 118
  states authorising, 14
  statewide, 100, 117
  unlimited, 21
  in U.S., 9
  widened, 47
  within district, 47
British Petroleum, 81
brokerage commissions, 76, 81, 83, 87
brokerage firms, 83
bull market, 84
bullion dealing, 79
Burns, Arthur F., 123
business practices, 19

California Bankers Assoc., 151
California expansion, 29–30
California Financial Code, 34
California State Banking Board, 57
Canadian Imperial Bank of Commerce, 38
Canadian province and municipal bonds, 27
capital controls, 60, 72, 152
  exception, 66
  imposed, 91
  removal, 41, 50, 60–1, 91, 106
capital flows, 22, 105–6, 120–1, 135, 136, 138, 140
capital funds, 139
capital market, 82, 83, 85, 86, 88, 92, 133, 135

Japan, 5
Swiss, 5
capital requirements, 96, 97
capital to deposit ratio, 153
cash collateral accounts, 28
CCB Group, 37
central banks, 58
central market system, 82
certificate of deposit (CD), 20, 58, 62, 65, 134
Chartered Bank of London, 101, 102
Chase Manhattan Bank, 12, 80, 107
Chicago Loop District, 48
clearing, 62, 63, 134
clearing balances, 65
clearing banks, 137
closed end trust, 80
collections, 28, 61
colonial empire, 126
commercial banking, 84
commercial and industrial loans, 24, 32, 41
commercial paper, 62
Commerzbank, 37
compensating balance, 71
competitive effects, 38, 148
complementary interests, 121
Comptroller of the Currency, 102, 112, 114, 123
concentration in banking, 148–9
Conference Board, 77
consortium banking, 42
consumer loans, 21, 30, 38
conversion to branches, 25
corporate trust activities, 40–1
correspondent, 10, 34
cost of funds, 63
County Bank, Santa Barbara, 49, 101
credit balances, 10, 28, 34, 98, 153
credit creation, 22
Crédit Lyonnais, 37
credit markets, 18, 50
credit risk, 90
credit squeeze, 21
creditor status of U.S., 11
currency
  dollar base, 21
  exposure, 66
  risk, 90
  role of dollar, 11, 18
  strength, 4
  swaps, 5
  vehicle, 134

INDEX

data processing, 38
de novo, 40, 96
dealer and broker profitability, 84
dealer organisation, 84, 90
debt securities, 84
Department of Justice, 103
Department of State, 97
deposit, 10
  CDs, 20, 29
  competition, 50–1
  concentration, 51–3
  demand, 62, 66, 150
  Eurodollar, 27
  foreign source, 14, 29
  functions, 98–9
  insurance, 10, 14, 29, 34
  London, 132–4
  offshore, 34
  savings, 150
  sources, 22
  structure, 51, 56
  time, 62, 66
deposit insurance costs, 34
depository function, 61–2
depression, 11
Deutsche Bank, 37
devaluation, dollar, 77
development finance, 79
dilution, 139
direct investment, 9, 18, 72
  controls, 91
  earnings, 78
  in U.K., 131
  in U.S., 77–9, 152
directors examinations, 99
discount window, 114, 124
dispersion of return, 73–6
Distillers Corp.–Seagrams, 81
diversification, 75–6, 99–100
dollar bonds, 86
dollar funds
  elasticity of supply, 63
  stable value, 134
dollar scarcity, 90
dollar sourcing, 20–1
draft, 11
Dresdner Bank, 37
dual banking, 18, 116
due from banks, 66, 99
Dwyer, William T., 151

economies of scale, 76
Edge Act Companies, 38, 111, 114, 115, 124
  interstate, 48, 140
  investment banking, 103
  multiple, 108
  out of state, 45, 118, 154
  potential, 110
efficient diversification, 75–6
Eisenhower administration, 90
entrepot, 136, 142
equal treatment approach, 123–4
equity capital, 87
equity investments, 111
equity securities, 81, 83, 84, 153
ethnic appeal, 21, 35
Eurobonds, 130
Eurocurrency
  borrowings, 105
  centres, 20
  deposits, 152
  flexibility, 66
  loans, 69
  London, 128, 130, 132, 134
  market, 5, 27, 50, 58
  oil funds, 88
  rate, 50, 71
Eurodollar, *see* Eurocurrency
EuroPartners Securities Corp., 37, 104
European American Bank & Trust, 26, 139, 151, 154
examinations, 99
exchange restrictions, 134, 135
Executive Order of the President, 12
expected return, 73–5
export–import trade, 3–4
  decline, 11
  financing, 19, 24, 28, 63, 79
  negative balance, 11
  with Japan, 27
  of U.S., 11

factoring, 49, 79
federal
  charter, 111–12, 124, 139
  funds, 20, 22, 27, 29, 58, 65
  licensing bill, 39
Federal Deposit Insurance Corp., 10
  acquisition, 101
  cost advantage, 65
  coverage, 108, 114, 119, 123
  jurisdiction, 102, 111
  premiums, 64
  required, 100, 115
  state chartered subsidiaries, 64

Federal Reserve
  acquisition, 102
  authorities, 50
  Board, 40, 66, 69, 102, 108, 111, 116
  denial, 104
  legislative proposal, 113–15
  membership, 10, 112, 114, 119, 123
  monetary policy, 50
  Steering Committee on International Banking, 113
  study of foreign banks, 39
  voluntary reserves, 69
Federal Reserve Bank of New York, 140
First National Bank of Chicago, 151
First National City Bank, 12, 107
First Pennsylvania Banking & Trust, 45
First Westchester National Bank, 38, 49
First Western Bank & Trust, 32, 39, 65, 101, 139, 151
fixed commissions, 83
float, 28
Florida statute, 102
foreign bank assets, 138, 145–6
Foreign Bank Control Act (Patman Bill), 110
foreign bank subsidiaries, 3
  in California, 29–30
  of Canadian banks, 5
  chartered, 95
  in New York, 25–6
  proposal, 111
  treatment, 14
  trust activities, 25
  in U.S., 9, 14
foreign bonds, 135
foreign currency
  deposits, 5
  funds, 135
foreign exchange, 5, 24, 27, 28, 32, 58, 63, 100, 153
foreign investment
  in U.S., 9
  inflow, 4, 5
  short-term, 9
Foreign Investment Study Act of 1974, 72
Foreign Office Banking Act, 101
foreign remittances, 24, 28
Franklin National Bank, 26, 90, 139, 140–1, 149, 151, 154

gap, regulatory, 95
German American Securities Corp., 37
Glass-Steagall Act, 22, 83, 84, 85, 102, 103, 120
gold, 58
gold reserves, 5
Grady, Stafford R., 151
grandfather protection, 115

head offices, 19, 21, 22, 27, 29, 60, 62, 63, 66, 69, 99
Hongkong and Shanghai Banking Corp., 11
Hunt Commission Report, 142

Industrial Bank of Japan, 26
institutional pressures, 115–22
interbank market, 22, 58, 71
Interest Equalization Tax, 60, 69, 82, 152
  removal, 86, 89, 91, 135
interest rates, 24
Inter-National Bank of Miami, 40, 102
International Holding Corp., 80
International Monetary Fund, 58
International Nickel, 81
interstate banking, 48–9
  effects, 56
  foreign banks, 107–8, 116, 123
  operations, 38, 108, 115, 121, 124, 140, 152, 154
interstate basis, 38
Intra Bank, 110, 153
investment adviser, 80, 86
investment banking, 50, 84, 108, 118, 141
investment companies, 10, 49, 98
Investment Company Act, 49
invisible earnings, 130–1

Japan-California Bank, 152
JFK Airport, 148
joint venture, 154

Kennedy administration, 91
KLM, 81
Korea Exchange Bank, 152

leasing, 49, 79
lending limits, 32
less developed countries, 9
letter of credit, 11, 27, 28, 30, 98
liberalised treatment, 124–5
Liberty National Bank, 101, 102
Life insurance, 49
listing, 81
liquidity adjustment, 57
Lloyds Bank Ltd, 32, 39, 65, 101, 139, 151

INDEX

loans
  brokers and dealers, 60
  call, 20
  commercial and industrial, 24, 32, 41
  corporate, 58, 79
  exempt from reserve requirements, 69
  flexibility, 63
  interest rate, 50
  intermediate, 130
  limits, 98
  local authorities, 134
  London branches, 71
  losses, 101
  low cost base, 63
  to non-residents, 61
  offshore, 50
  participation, 151
  restrictions, 96, 98
  syndicate, 50
local authorities, 134
London
  advantages, 128–30
  American banks, 126–7
  capital market, 133, 135
  deposit structure, 127, 132–4
  financial centre, 126
  foreign banks, 126, 127, 132
  money market, 133, 134
  stock exchange, 130, 135
London Interbank Offer Rate (LIBO), 63, 71, 106, 152
Long Island Trust Co., 38, 39, 107, 147–50, 154
Lorie Report, 82, 83

McFadden Act, 136, 154
merchant bank, 79, 85, 129, 148
merger, 100, 101, 112, 139
merger movement, 77
Merrill, Lynch, Pierce, Fenner & Smith, 80
military occupation, 86
monetary policy, 50, 104–5, 111, 113, 116, 138, 140
money market, 3, 4, 21, 22, 26
  activities, 9, 20, 40
  foreign banks, 62
  information, 20
  international orientation, 57–60
  London, 133–4
  New York, 5, 20
  ownership, 58–9
  pressures, 24, 58, 60
  size, 58–9
  size comparisons, 60, 134–5
money transfer, 62, 79
money trust, 85
monopolistic imperfections, 77
monopoly, 119, 139, 141
moral suasion, 69
mortgage company, 40, 49
multinational corporation, 69
mutual funds, 40, 86

National Bank of North America, 149
nationalisation, 39
nationwide banking, 46
near banking, 38, 48, 114, 121
  approved by Board, 49
  gain entry, 107
negative correlation, 76
negotiable certificate of deposit, 20
new issues, 40, 84, 90, 142
New York assets, 97, 99
New York Banking Law
  amendment of 1951, 12
  branching bill 1960, 12, 24
  revision of 1911, 11
New York Stock Exchange, 81, 82, 83, 84, 135, 153
NYSE study, 153
non-banking acquisition, 103, 124
non-conforming activities, 115, 124

Office of Foreign Direct Investment, 66, 69
official reserves, 61
oil energy crisis, 41
OPEC nations, 87, 88
open door, 136, 137
open economy, Canada, 5
overdrafts, 20
overlapping jurisdiction, 95
overseas branches, 111
ownership restrictions, 46

Pacific Basin, 100
Patman, Wright, 39
Patman Bill, 110–13
personal checking, 21, 30
petro-dollar, 40, 41, 70, 87–90, 142
populist banking, 122
portfolio investment, 72, 108, 131
portfolio management, 9, 24, 29, 49, 72, 76, 80, 85–6
portfolio manager, 5

prime rate, 50, 63, 71, 106, 152
prospectus, 50
protectionist policy, 39

real estate company, 40
reciprocal branching, 109, 113, 118, 125, 141
reciprocity, 12, 82, 84, 96, 106–7, 119, 120, 121, 124, 140, 148, 154
Rees bill, 113
regional exchanges, 82, 153
regulation
  alternatives, 122–5
  California, 100–1
  capital requirements, 97–8
  de novo operations, 96–7
  federal, 102–4
  Florida, 101–2
  Illinois, 101
  new proposals, 104, 110–15, 139
  New York State, 96–100
  present system, 95–7
  problems, 104–10
Regulation D, 69
Regulation M, 69
Regulation Y, 80
regulatory environment, 4
remittance, 79
representative offices, 9, 17
  cost of, 34
  disadvantages, 34
  functions, 10, 33
  interstate, 48, 152
  licensing, 14, 33
  number, 14
reserve adjustment, 66
reserve in IMF, 58
reserve requirements, 34
  as cost factor, 64
  equalise, 123
  foreign banks, 105, 114
  member banks, 65
  nature of, 99
  New York, 108
  offshore funds, 66, 69, 71
  state comparisons, 65–8
  state nonmember banks, 65
  voluntary, 69
restrictive approach, 122–3
retail banking, 9, 10, 21, 24, 29, 39, 40, 41, 147, 148
Revenue Act of 1962, 91
risk-return relation, 74, 77

Roan Selection Trust, 81
Rothschild, Baron Edmond de, 101
Royal Trust Co. of Montreal, 40, 102

Sanwa Bank Ltd, 20
savings account, 21
Schlumberger, 81
Schroder, Naess & Thomas, 79–80
Schroder, J. Henry, Banking Corp., 80
Schroder Trust Company, 80
SDRs, 58
securities affiliates, 79, 85, 86, 87, 90, 114, 119, 120, 123
Securities Exchange Commission, 77, 83, 87
securities market linkages, 21–2
securities safekeeping, 86
Security National Bank, 147, 149
separate entity, 153
Sony, 81
Southern California First National Bank, 101, 151
speciality finance, 79
stage of economic development, 3
standard deviation, 74, 153
state laws, 14
status quo, 122
sterling, 58
  deposits, 126, 128
  exchange restrictions, 134–5
  market, 132
  reserve currency, 126
  weak currency, 129, 134
sterling area, 135
stock brokerage, 115, 118
stock market, 9, 36, 40, 77, 79, 82, 83, 84, 104, 118, 130
strategic industry, 107
strategy approaches, 36
structure of banking, 45
  changes, 46–7, 109, 124, 140, 142
  comparison, 131–3
  competitive, 45, 111, 124–5
  differences, 118
  foreign banks, 50–1
  non-competing, 45
  periodic review, 142
suasion, 95, 99
Sumitomo Bank of Calif., 65
supervisory powers, 99–100
swap, 27
Swiss American Corp., 37
Swiss Bank Corp., 37

Swiss Credit Bank, 37
Swiss franc, 5
synergy, 76, 152

takeover bids, 110
tax strategy, 69
tiered interest rate, 141
Tokai Bank of Calif., 152
tombstone prospectus, 50
trading companies, borrowing requirements, 32
trading firms, 77
transaction costs, 76
transfer taxes, 76
Truman administration, 90
trust company, 10, 26, 49, 97, 98, 99, 102
trust department, 86
trust funds, 87

UBS-DB Corporation, 37
underwriting, 5, 9, 21, 37, 79, 80, 81, 82, 86, 90, 103, 104, 115, 118, 120
 outside U.S., 36
 prohibitions, 22
Unilever, 81
Union Bank of Switzerland, 37
unit banking, 47–8, 55, 101, 117, 119
U.S. government securities, 24, 66, 88

variance of return, 74
vault cash, 65, 66
venture capital, 10, 79, 85, 142
voluntary controls, 69

Wall Street, 86
Wall Street Journal, 50
weak banks, 139
wholesale banking, 40
withholding tax, removal, 91
World Airways Inc., 39
World War I, 11
World War II, 12, 126